HAYMARKET REVISITED

by William Adelman

A Tour Guide of Labor History
Sites and Ethnic Neighborhoods
Connected with the Haymarket Affair

Second in a Series
**Published by
The Illinois Labor History Society**

Completed:
Touring Pullman

Other projected titles:
The Chicago Loop and Labor History
The West Side and "Union Row"
Pilsen and the Railroad Strike of 1877
The Virden Riot and Southern Illinois
The South Side and Memorial Day Massacre

Cover and Maps: Designed by
  William Neebe and executed by
  Susan Misch and Janice Rajecki of
  the Graphics Arts Studio of the Chicago
  Circle Campus of the University of
  Illinois.

1976
The Illinois Labor History Society
2800 Sheridan Road
Chicago, Ill. 60657

Library of Congress No. 75-10016
IBSN 0-916884-03-1

Printed in U.S.A.
Moore Langen Co.
Terre Haute, Indiana

INTRODUCTION

On Tuesday, May 4, 1886 at half past eight in the evening a crowd of about 2,500 people gathered around an old delivery wagon parked on Desplaines Street near Haymarket Square in Chicago. August Spies, a labor newspaper editor, stood on the wagon as he protested against what had happened the day before when police shot down striking workers at the McCormick Reaper Plant. Next Albert Parsons, a labor leader, spoke, and he was followed by Samuel Fielden, a Methodist lay-preacher and community leader. Each of the men outlined what was wrong with American society. As Fielden was about to finish his speech about half past ten, a formation of 176 armed policemen attacked the crowd that had by then dwindled down to only about 200. Suddenly, a dynamite bomb was thrown by someone unknown. It was the first time such a device was ever used in the United States. The bomb landed in the middle of the police, killing one man and seriously injuring dozens of others. The police shot into the crowd killing at least four workers and wounding more than a score of others. In their panic the police killed some of their own men. Eventually six more policemen would die.

For the next several weeks freedom of speech and assembly ended in Chicago and other cities throughout the country. Hundreds of labor and ethnic community leaders were arrested. The Knights of Labor was blamed for the violence and the newspapers, business, and eventually the public turned against labor unions and everyone cried for "law and order." Eventually eight men were brought to trial and four of them were hung on November 11, 1887. On the day before, one of the men, Louis Lingg, was found in his cell with his face half blown away by a dynamite cap. Some would say he committed suicide; others would say he had been murdered by the police.

In June of 1893 the Governor of Illinois, John Peter Altgeld, pardoned the three survivors and thereby risked his own political future.

The Haymarket meeting, the throwing of the bomb or so-called "Haymarket Riot," the trial, execution, and the events that followed are known as "The Haymarket Affair."

The Haymarket Affair of 1886 occurred a long time ago, and may seem to some an event reserved for the history books. But, the issues that led to the Haymarket Affair are problems that are still with us today. . .unemployment, the rights of minority groups, a fair distribution of wealth, freedom of speech and assembly, political corruption, police surveillance and brutality, and the right of American workers to organize unions of their choice.

Although Chicago has changed a great deal since 1886 and many of the old buildings have been demolished, there is still a great deal to see in visiting the sites connected with Haymarket.

Haymarket Square is still very much the same. The old Cook County Court House and the area where the County Jail once stood still have the look and feel of the 1880's. The Wicker Park-Milwaukee Avenue area is filled with beautiful architecture and exciting ethnic neighborhoods. And a visit to old German Waldheim Cemetery can not help but move you to appreciate the tragedy of the Haymarket Affair. You will be impressed not only with the dramatic lives of the Haymarket Eight but also with those twenty-four other people whose destinies were changed by the Haymarket Meeting, the Trial, and the Execution.

Few events have had more significance than Haymarket, yet few Americans realize its importance. This book is written especially for the working men and women of America who need to look again at this turning point in American labor history.

WHY DID IT HAPPEN IN CHICAGO?

In the 1950's the Chicago writer, Nelson Algren, called Chicago the "city on the make", a place were "it's every man for himself. . ." It seems that Chicago was this way from the very beginning. Chicago was not a cooperative society but a highly competitive one. Foreign visitors in the 1880's said that Chicagoans "generally are so engrossed in pursuing their business enterprises and piling up fortunes that there is little time to think of much else." The usual comment by foreigners was that "the dollar is king in Chicago."

Chicago was by the 1880's the fastest growing city in the world. The kind of people it attracted were the kind that were out for themselves. The London Times in 1887 said Chicago "contains probably more of the speculative, extravagant, shrewd, and reckless elements of American humanity than even New York".

Those who came to Chicago early naturally had the greatest opportunity to achieve success, since land was cheap and everything still had to be built. The early Anglo-Saxon Protestants like George Pullman, Marshall Field, Potter Palmer, and Cyrus McCormick, who came from New England and the East, dominated the life of the city throughout the second half of the 19th century. Their heirs continued to control the city politically until the 1930's.

The Irish immigrants who came in the 1830's and 1840's, and the Germans who began to come after 1848 were regarded as inferior by the earlier settlers. They were regarded as cheap labor to be exploited. When the Irish and Germans began to organize and fight for their rights as American citizens, Czech, Bohemian, Polish and other ethnic workers were brought in and played against them. Consequently, racial and ethnic conflict became an early characteristic of Chicago.

The wealthy businessmen of the city would not face the problems they had created for their workers. They wanted to believe that their workers could become rich just as they had. When thousands were unemployed the rich immediately assumed that the poor must be lazy. A year before Haymarket an anonymous Chicago businessman wrote an article titled "Hard Times and How to Mend Them", which gave the following paternalistic advice to the poor ethnic workers:

"Comparatively small wages, if properly husbanded, will soon make you and yours independent. . .It requires no particular heroism, no superior wisdom, or exceptional energy, to achieve independence. Industry, temperance, and good management are the watchwords. . ."

But how could a man earning only about a dollar a day put anything aside? How could the woman or child earning only 5¢ an hour follow this advice? By the 1880's new machinery was destroying the jobs of even skilled workers, and with an ever increasing supply of surplus labor in Chicago there was always someone to take your place if you wouldn't accept a wage cut or longer hours.

THE POLITICAL SUPPRESSION OF MINORITY GROUPS IN CHICAGO

By 1855 there were more foreign-born voters in Chicago than native-born. The rich businessmen of the city were afraid of losing political control of the city and they organized a racist, anti-foreigner, anti-worker political party known as the Know-Nothings.

Dr. Levi D. Boone, an ultra-conservative physician, was chosen as the mayoral candidate, and he pledged to purify city hall by firing all foreigners from all city jobs, the police department, and the fire department. He also enforced the Sunday closing laws against the saloons and beer gardens and raised the liquor licensing fees from $30 to $300 a year. These saloons and beer gardens were the meeting places of the Irish and German workers on their only day off, Sunday. Freedom of speech and assembly could not be prevented under the Constitution but closing the drinking establishments on Sunday was the next best thing.

Early in the morning of April 21, 1855 and again that afternoon at 3 p.m., German workers tried to march from the German neighborhoods on Milwaukee Avenue into the downtown area to demonstrate around the city hall. Mayor Boone placed gatling guns on city hall to cover 75% of the approaches into the downtown area and he swore in over 250 vigilantes from the businessmen of the city to supplement the police force. In the afternoon when they tried to cross the Clark Street bridge, Mayor Boone ordered the bridge turned, trapping the Germans on the bridge in the middle of the river. The police then opened fire, wounding many Germans and killing Steve Martin, a 26 year old worker. Only one policeman, Officer Hunt, was injured. When he lost his left arm from gangrene the businessmen took up a collection and gave him $3,000 for saving Chicago from the Huns. An investigation of this "riot" was made, and the mayor himself later admitted his mistake. The investigating committee recommended that more German, Scandinavian, Irish, and other foreign speaking police be used in ethnic neighborhoods to promote better understanding and unity in the city.

A Vigilante Committee attacking workers near 18th and Ashland Avenue.

THE GREAT FIRE, UNEMPLOYMENT, AND STARVATION

The Chicago Fire left over 100,000 people homeless and 250 known dead. Many of the homeless were the ethnic German and Scandinavian workers who lived along Chicago Avenue and next to the Chicago River. These groups also suffered the largest number of fatalities, since they were trapped in their homes between the main fire and the spark ignited lumber yards that lined the river.

After the fire, workers throughout the United States as well as citizens in England, France, and Germany donated over five million dollars for the relief of the starving people of Chicago (this would be half a billion in terms of today's buying power). Instead of administrating this money through city agencies, Mayor Medill turned the funds over to the Relief and Aid Society that was made up of many of his business friends.

At first the money was given to the poor, but later the starving workers found it more and more difficult to get relief. The Director of the Chicago Relief and Aid Society said:

"We are not to blame if people have not looked closely enough after their own interest to be out of work and money now, and these people have no right to demand that money of us."

The period after the Civil War was a difficult time for workers all over the country, but more difficult for Chicago workers because of the fire and dishonest employers. Many workers in construction didn't even receive pay for work performed, since some contractors refused to honor their commitment. There was not even a law requiring workers to be paid. Native-born workers spread the word about such contractors, but newly arrived and hungry immigrant workers were often taken in.

During the winter of 1872, thousands of these starving workers marched on the Relief and Aid Society for money to buy food, but instead they were driven into a tunnel under the Chicago River, where they were clubbed and beaten. This would be known in the history of Chicago as the "Bread Riot" (See No. 29 for more details).

The Bread Riot, Winter 1872, northeast corner of LaSalle and Randolph (Courtesy of Chicago Historical Society)

A new arrival to Chicago named Albert Parsons would investigate this situation, and finally the State of Illinois ordered an investigation of its own. It was discovered that the administrators of the funds were borrowing money from the fund at no interest rather than going to the banks. They were using the funds for their businesses instead of giving the money to the poor. Since no law against such actions existed at that time, none of them were ever prosecuted.

The period from the Civil War to 1886 was a period of "boom and bust" for Chicago with at least ten years of economic disaster and depression. Even the construction industry fell off as the city was rebuilt. An investigation by the Bureau of Labor Statistics in 1880 showed that half the salary of a worker was going for food.

As the unemployment increased, efforts were made to send the surplus labor out to work on the farms around Chicago. A member of the Relief Society Administration told a group of unemployed workers that their condition was inexcusable and that they "ought to have money in the bank to stand a two years' panic if necessary."

The cycles of the economy, the seasonal nature of many jobs, and the abundance of cheap foreign labor, made unemployment and destitution a way of life in Chicago. This was in sharp contrast to the great fortunes that were being made at the same time by men like George Pullman, Armour, Swift, Marshall Field, and Potter Palmer.

THE RAILROAD STRIKE OF 1877 AND MILITANT ACTION

Although the "Bread Riot" of the Winter of 1872 had shown the workers of Chicago the indifference of the rich toward their plight, it was not until July of 1877 that the workers again tried militant action.

They had tried political action for several years, running men like Albert Parsons for political office, but the lack of a secret ballot in Illinois, coercion by employers of their employees at election time, and the stuffing of ballot boxes against liberal candidates caused many to become discouraged with the democratic process. By 1877, the workers were taking to the streets, and the business community was trembling in fear. These fears were fanned by the newspapers, especially the new Daily News and the Tribune, that exaggerated the reports of what was happening.

The Strike of 1877 started in the East in West Virginia and Pennsylvania. It reached Chicago the morning of Monday, July 23 when employees of the Michigan Central Railroad in its yards at Randolph and Michigan Avenue walked out. By the following day workers were walking off the job all over Chicago. Streetcars were not running on the southside, ships sat in their moorings along the river as sailors went on strike, and 8,000 workers gathered at the Chicago, Burlington, and Quincy Roundhouse on the southwestside. The police dispersed the 8,000 workers by killing three of them and wounding seven.

That same evening workers gathered in Market Square (see site 15) for a torchlight rally. Albert Parsons gave a moderate but exciting speech that united ethnic and native-born workers in a way they had never been united before. Parsons called for workingmen to join the Workingmen's Party and to exercise the ballot to obtain State control of transportation, communication, and certain means of production and get them "out of the hands or control of private individuals, corporations, monopolists, and syndicates." The speech was listened to with great enthusiasm and the meeting of about 6,000 people was very orderly.

The next morning, Tuesday, July 24 Parsons was fired by his employer the Chicago Times and blacklisted by that paper for addressing the Market Square Meeting. When Parsons went to the Chicago Tribune to look for a job as a typographer he was thrown down two flights of stairs by two thugs who were probably under orders of Joseph Medill, editor and former Chicago mayor, whom Parsons had embarrassed by his 1874 investigation of the "Bread Riot".

On the afternoon of July 24th, while trying to get a job setting type at one of the German ethnic newspapers located on the Market Square, he was approached by several plainclothesmen who asked him to come to the temporary City-Hall (located in the original Rookery Building at Adams and LaSalle). There he was told by the police and fifty members of the Board of Trade to leave town or he would be hung from the nearest lamp post. They screamed out things like, "Hang him," "Lynch him," "Lock him up."

Two days later on Thursday, July 26, more troops arrived in Chicago. While the 1st Regiment of the Illinois National Guard had been in the city for several days, they were now supplemented by Federal troops from the Dakotas who only days before had been used against the Indians that had killed General Custer. These troops were now used against Chicago workers at 16th Street and Halsted, in what the history books call "The Battle of the Viaduct."

The "Battle of the Viaduct"

The police raided union halls and again interfered with the rights of freedom of speech and assembly throughout the city. On the same day as the "Battle of the Viaduct", July 26, the police showed their lack of respect for individual rights by breaking down the door of the Westside Turner Hall at Roosevelt and Halsted. This event was described sixteen years later by Governor Altgeld in his pardon of the remaining Haymarket Martyrs as illustrative of the way the police exceeded their authority. The Furniture-Workers Union was meeting with their employers to discuss wages and the eight-hour day, and they had received a permit for their meeting from the City of Chicago. Despite official permission, the police raided the hall, clubbed and fired upon the men as they struggled to escape from the building, killing a worker named Tessman, and wounding many others.

The union took the case to the courts, and the judge was forced to find the Chicago Police Department guilty since the workers had a city permit. The police were fined a dollar and this prevented an appeal to a higher court.

Police attacking workers at the Westside Turner Hall (Roosevelt and Halsted)

In order to sell newspapers, stories were written to excite the public. The reports of riots were exaggerated, deaths were sometimes increased seven-fold in the news stories, and the inhumane attitude and fears of the business community were reflected in the newspaper editorials.

The Chicago Times advocated the use of dynamite against strikers. A "Law and Order League" was formed with George Pullman as its head. Marshall Field armed the clerks in his store and gave his delivery wagons to the troops and police for the movement of forces around the city. Albert Parsons was proclaimed by the newspapers as a "wanted man" although they had nothing to arrest him for. Victor Lawson and his newly founded Daily News made a fortune by scaring the public.

The rich of Chicago felt that the world was coming to an end and their way of life about to be destroyed. Surrounded by troops in the Exposition Building (once on the site of the present Art Institute) the rich gathered during the strike to hear a concert by Theodore Thomas and his orchestra. Maestro Thomas played music by Wagner, and he played very loudly to drown out the noise of the troops marching up Michigan Avenue. Years later one Chicago businessman who gave a great deal of money for the construction of Orchestra Hall, said that for at least that evening he felt that his society was safe and that life might again return to normal.

Life in Chicago did return to normal after the defeat of the strike in early August. However, the Railroad Strike of 1877 taught the workers of Chicago three things. They needed more political action in order to fight "The Establishment" of the city. They needed ethnic newspapers to tell their side of the story, since they could not trust the major city papers. Many workers also believed they needed military groups of their own for protection from future police attacks. The years from 1877 to 1886 would see both success and failure in carrying out these three ventures.

POLITICAL ACTION, WORKER NEWSPAPERS, AND THE ORGANIZATION OF MILITARY GROUPS

The Workingmen's Party again ran candidates in the elections of 1878, 1879, and 1880. Frank Stauber ran in the 14th Ward, a German working-class neighborhood, and the election was stolen from him by means of ballot-box stuffing. The same thing happened to Parsons when he ran for Alderman of Chicago from the 15th Ward. Although a judge recognized that there were many irregularities in the election, he refused to call for a new election. Later Parsons said the following:

"It was then I began to realize the hopeless task of political reformation. Many workingmen began to lose faith in the potency of the ballot or the protection of the law for the poor. . . ."

The workers had more success in the establishment of worker newspapers. On March 22, 1879, a giant rally was held in the Exposition Hall on Michigan Avenue and over 40,000 people came to hear Albert Parsons and August Spies speak. Enough money was raised to buy the Arbeiter-Zeitung newspaper and run it as a German language worker paper. Parsons also helped to establish a similar English language paper, The Alarm. Besides these daily papers several German weekly papers were also founded. . . the Vorbote, and Die Fackel. Although none of these papers had a huge circulation, they were effective in presenting the Chicago workers' point of view until they were shut down by the police after the Haymarket bombing on May 4, 1886.

Many workers were determined after the Railroad Strike of 1877 that never again would they be shot down by the police or U. S. troops during rallies or strikes; nor would they see their wives and children beaten. Knowing that the Constitution of the United States guaranteed them "the right to bear arms", each ethnic group set up "gun clubs" in order to protect themselves. Among these "gun clubs" was an English Club for native-born workers, The German Club (Lehr and Wehr Verein), the Bohemian Sharpshooters, and even a French group.

In March of 1879 many of these groups took part in a march up State Street, and drilled in Grant Park to show off their military ability. These demonstrations were too much for "The Establishment" of Chicago. In April of 1879 a bill was pushed through the State General Assembly outlawing the right of these workers to carry arms. The new law was written in such a way that only the police and the Illinois National Guard could carry guns. Many of the businessmen of the city were officers in the National Guard and were therefore still able to carry arms.

This law was immediately contested by the workingmen. The case was carried to the Supreme Court of the United States, where it was decided that the State Legislatures of the United States had a constitutional right to disarm the workingmen. Many of the "gun clubs" were dissolved; others went underground. There was a great deal of debate among the workers in Chicago as to what they might do if the police and the military again used their weapons illegally against them.

THE "POOR PEOPLES' MARCH" OF 1884 AND THE "MARCH AGAINST THE BOARD OF TRADE" IN 1885

The President of the United States and Governor Oglesby of Illinois both signed declarations establishing Nov. 25, 1884 as a Day of Thanksgiving. But many of the workers of Chicago felt they had nothing to be thankful for. It was decided that instead they would organize a "Poor People's March" to go through the neighborhoods of the rich, ringing door bells and demanding jobs.

The march started in the Market Square in downtown Chicago and proceeded through the southside by the homes of George Pullman, Marshall Field, Swift, Armour, and others along Prairie Avenue. Later they passed along Rush Street on the northside by the homes of Cyrus McCormick and former Ambassador to France, E. B. Washburne, who had publicly condemned worker demonstrations in France during his term as ambassador.

George Pullman was supposedly so disgusted with these hundreds of poor people, led by Albert Parsons and his black wife Lucy, that he had a meeting the next morning with his attorney, Wirt Dexter. There were reports throughout the city that George Pullman, Chairman of the Law and Order League, was determined to get Albert Parsons and have him thrown into jail.

By 1885, there was still more unemployment in Chicago, and again honest, respectable workingmen were driven to desperation. At the same time the members of the Board of Trade were planning a twenty dollar a plate dinner for the opening of the new two million dollar Board of Trade Building at the south end of LaSalle Street.

Parsons, Rev. Samuel Fielden, and several of the other Haymarket Martyrs took part in a "March Against the Board of Trade" on April, 28, 1885. Parsons spoke to the group from the front of the Arbeiter-Zeitung offices on Wells Street (See No. 87) saying, "How many of my hearers could give twenty dollars for a supper tonight?...While those men are enjoying a sumptuous supper, workingmen are starving."

Parsons went on to say..."They amass hundreds of millions of dollars by manipulating railroad, mine, telegraph, oil and other stocks...They create panics, bring about business and commercial stagnations for the purpose of enriching themselves...we have an example of what they do when we recollect that Philip Armour, of the Chicago Board of Trade, realized a million and a half dollars in twenty-four hours by manipulating the pork market last summer."

After Parsons spoke, the workers marched around the new Board of Trade Building carrying red and black flags and union banners. The march was led by Oscar Neebe and Lucy Parsons. The police formed a line around the building to protect the rich dinner guests who were alighting from their carriages to enter the magnificent new building. Although there was one minor incident of rock throwing, the march was nonviolent. The police under Inspector Welter showed good judgment on this occasion.

MORE POLICE BRUTALITY DURING THE STREETCAR STRIKE OF 1885

Several incidents of police brutality took place during a strike of streetcar workers in late June and early July of 1885. The Conductors and Drivers Union under the leadership of its president, Brother Klechner, was demanding shorter hours, equalization of pay, and an end to harassment of union members.

Instead of discussing the problems with the workers, Mr. Lake, President of the West Division Streetcar Company, permanently discharged sixteen of the key union men. Lake also held a secret meeting with the Pinkerton Detective Agency and Captain Bonfield of the Desplaines Street Police Station. While the Mayor of Chicago, Carter Harrison, had ordered the Chicago Police Department to stay out of the dispute, Captain Bonfield openly opposed the Mayor and offered his policeman as strikebreakers.

On Wednesday, July 1st when Pinkertons and policemen tried to run streetcars along Madison Street into the downtown area, they were met by a mob of men, women, and children at the corner of Halsted and Madison Streets. The mob derailed the streetcar and turned it over. They objected not only to the police trying to break the strike, but to the whole streetcar system run by the "Streetcar King", Charles Yerkes, who overcharged the workers, refused to give transfers, and underpaid his employees.

Captain Bonfield struck back with terrible brutality. The police clubbed and beat everyone in sight including Madison Street owners, who had stepped out on the sidewalk to see what was happening, and gas company workers, who were digging up part of the street for a new gas line.

On July 6 the company finally agreed to arbitration through the Mayor of Chicago. But Captain Bonfield continued to harass the public by issuing a "shoot to kill" order on July 7 and by leading 400 policeman out to the Westside. Bonfield personally tried to shoot a worker named Peter Steflin, who was throwing rocks at a scab-run streetcar; but Bonfield missed. Steflin, however, was arrested and thrown into jail. By the fall of 1885, the businessmen of Chicago were trying to get Bonfield appointed as the Superintendent of Police for the entire City of Chicago. The Trades and Labor Assembly and the other unions of the city strongly opposed Bonfield's appointment. Although he never became superintendent, he was appointed Inspector of Police and assigned to the Central Police Headquarters in City Hall.

As Inspector of Police, Bonfield began a city-wide campaign of drilling his men in new techniques of riot control. Lucy Parsons wrote an article about this in the Alarm on December 21, 1885.

"Let us examine into this matter and ascertain, if we can, what this streetriot drill is for. Certainly not for the purpose of fighting enemies from without; nor for a foreign foe, for if this was the case we would be massing our armies on the seacoast. Then it must be for our enemies within...Then who is the street-riot drill for? For whom is it intended? Who is to be shot?"

CAPTAIN BONFIELD AND THE STRIKE AT THE McCORMICK REAPER PLANT

While many Chicago businesses were expanding in the years after the Civil War, none grew more rapidly or became better known than the McCormick Harvesting Machine Company (known today as the International Harvester Company).

When old Cyrus McCormick and his brother Leander McCormick first founded the company there was close relationship between the owners and the workers. But as the plant grew, relationships became more impersonal. During a foundry strike in 1862 the union first appeared at the plant and was accepted. Through the Molders' Union Local 23 many of the workers in the plant were provided with some democracy on the job.

Dramatic changes began to take place in the plant management after Leander McCormick left the firm. Then in 1884 Cyrus McCormick died suddenly. The management of the plant was turned over to the twenty-five year old Cyrus McCormick II, who had very little experience. The young McCormick was determined to break the union, cut wages and piecework by 10-15%, and increase the profits of the company. Although there was a depression in Chicago in 1884-85, the McCormick Company was still making a profit of 71% yearly on an investment of 2 1/2 million dollars.

The timing of this pay cut was very bad since it came at the very time that the newspapers were announcing that the McCormick family intended to give another $100,000 to the Chicago Presbyterian Theological Seminary (making a total in contributions of over $450,000). Today this seminary is known as the McCormick Theological Seminary and still occupies a large site on the southwest corner of Halsted and Fullerton.

Workers at the McCormick Plant, many of whom were Catholics, figured that their wage cuts were paying for all of the contributions to this Presbyterian school. A series of strikes and lockouts began in 1884 and continued until May of 1886. It was a confrontation between workers, strikebreakers, and the police under Captain Bonfield on May 3, 1886 at the McCormick Plant that led to the Haymarket Protest Meeting on May 4th.

Why had relations at the McCormick Plant between workers and management gotten so serious by May 3, 1886 at the time of the nation-wide marches for the eight-hour day? How did Captain Bonfield become Inspector of Police?

After the donations to the seminary in 1885 a strike took place at the main plant in Chicago's Pilsen neighborhood. Young McCormick decided to use Pinkerton Detectives and scabs to try to break the strike of the Molders' Union. McCormick hoped to use the police, as well, but an Irishman, Captain O'Donnell, was the captain in the Pilsen neighborhood, and he refused to allow his men to be used against the Irish and other ethnic workers at the plant.

Even the general public was against the tactics of young McCormick; and the older and wiser Philip Armour advised McCormick to give in to the union demands. Although McCormick was finally forced to rehire the workers at their original pay scale, he was more determined than ever to break the union in the plant.

McCormick felt that the one factor contributing to his loss of the 1885 strike was lack of support from the Chicago Police Department. McCormick decided to use his influence to have Captain O'Donnell, the neutral Irish policeman, replaced by Captain Bonfield, who was known for his anti-labor, anti-foreigner prejudices.

Inspector Bonfield

Captain Bonfield had particularly impressed businessmen like McCormick because of his "shoot to kill order" during the Streetcar Strike in 1885. Bonfield also impressed the business community with his willingness to work closely with the Pinkerton Detective Agency. Many other businessmen besides McCormick were beginning to see the advantage of using the police and the Pinkertons to break the unions existing within their plants.

In October of 1885, the Pinkerton Detective Agency circulated a letter to businessmen throughout the country. It read as follows:

"At this time, when there is so much dissatisfaction among the labor classes and secret labor societies are organizing throughout the United States, we suggest . . . for railroad companies and other corporations . . . to keep a close watch for designing men among their own employees, who . . . are influencing their employees to join these organizations and eventually cause a strike. It is frequently the case that, by taking a matter of this kind, and discovering the ring-leaders, and dealing promptly with them, serious trouble may be avoided in the future."

After Bonfield became Inspector of Police, he proved very useful to young Cyrus McCormick. On February 16, 1886, McCormick locked out some 1,482 employees, many of whom were members of the Molders' Union Local 23. This time the Chicago Police Department under Bonfield assisted the company and over 300 policemen were stationed around the McCormick Reaper Plant. Everything was quiet until March 1, when, with the help of the police, strikebreakers were escorted into the plant to begin operations.

On March 2, the police charged a peaceable meeting of the locked-out men, who had assembled to discuss the situation and without warning, they clubbed the men and placed them under arrest. When some of the men ran and others resisted arrest the police opened fire; they continued to shoot rapidly at the fleeing men as long as they were in range. At least four men were killed.

John Peter Altgeld in discussing the events of March 2, 1886 stated that "this was wanton and unprovoked murder, and there was not even so much as an investigation." Altgeld regarded the developments at the McCormick Plant as the principal reason for the growing hatred between the police and the workers.

As he put it:

"... it is shown that various attempts were made to bring to justice the men who wore the uniform of the law while violating it, but all to no avail... the laboring people found the prisons always open to receive them..."

The lock-out at the McCormick Plant had already been going on for two and a half months when the "Eight Hour Day Movement" began on May 1, 1886. At a meeting at Grief's Hall Sunday, May 2, two lumberworkers asked August Spies, editor of the Arbeiter-Zeitung, if he would speak to a group of striking lumberworkers near the McCormick Plant on the afternoon of Monday, May 3. Spies agreed to speak.

Police sketch of the scene at the McCormick Reaper Plant on Monday May 3, 1886

Spies spoke to the 6000 workers from the top of a railroad freight car, but many in the audience were Polish and Bohemian and didn't understand a word he was saying. When the 3:30 bell went off at the nearby McCormick Plant some of the audience (about 200) left to help the locked-out workers heckle the scabs as they left the plant during the shift change. Almost immediately Bonfield and about 200 policemen arrived and a skirmish developed. This attracted more of Spies' audience. In fact, Spies himself decided to go over to find out what was happening. He and the rest of the crowd were greeted with clubs and a hail of bullets.

Spies was shocked by the police attack, and he took a streetcar back to the Arbeiter-Zeitung office on Wells Street to write a flyer condemning this latest example of police brutality. He had heard that two people were killed, which was the true figure, but when he picked up a copy of the Chicago Daily News the paper reported six deaths and he used this figure in his flyer. It is ironic that Spies would later be held responsible during the trial for exciting the workers with a false report of the number of dead. The judge would not even allow copies of the Daily News to be submitted as evidence.

On the evening of Monday, May 3, a group of workers that included Gottfried Waller and George Engel met in what the police later called the "Monday Night Conspiracy Meeting." It was proposed that a meeting take place in Haymarket Square on Tuesday, May 4 to protest what had been happening at the McCormick Reaper Plant, especially the attack by the police on May 3. Although August Spies would later be asked to speak at the Haymarket meeting, he had no part in its planning.

The events at the McCormick Reaper Plant, the union busting campaign of Chicago businessmen, and the anti-union activities of Bonfield and the Chicago Police Department were at their height at the same time that workers all over the United States were dedicating themselves to a nationwide strike for the "Eight Hour Day."

ORIGINS OF THE "EIGHT HOUR DAY MOVEMENT"-- MAY DAY, 1886

Workers in the United States had been fighting since the days of Andrew Jackson's Administration for shorter working hours. Under President Van Buren, federal employees won the ten hour day. The government was expected to be a model for the private sector, but private employers refused to follow voluntarily the government's example. Workers found they had to strike each individual employer to win the shorter hours.

During the post-Civil War recession, workers felt it would help the economy and that more people could be employed if everyone worked shorter hours at the same pay. The "Eight Hour Day Movement" was seen as a way of spreading the work around and helping people who had lost their jobs to the new labor saving machines. Under President Andrew Johnson, a new law was passed reducing the hours of work of federal employees to eight. In Illinois the General Assembly in March of 1867 passed a law declaring eight hours to be the "legal work day in the State of Illinois." These laws were not enforced and workers were forced to continue their fight for the right to the eight hour day.

Probably the first connection between May Day and the "Eight Hour Day Movement" was in Chicago in 1867. The

Molders' Union Local 23 at the McCormick Plant, which at the time was one of the strongest unions in the city, promoted a number of large demonstrations for the eight hour day throughout the city. Over 10,000 trade union workers left their jobs and marched through the streets. The Chicago Times called this the "largest procession ever seen on the streets of Chicago." Although some factories gave their employees the eight hour day, others refused and there were more strikes. Since this was a time of serious unemployment, workers from other cities came into Chicago as strikebreakers. As a result, the 1867 "Eight Hour Day Movement" failed and the ten, twelve, and fourteen hour day became the rule.

Meeting in Chicago in 1884, the Federation of Organized Trade and Labor Unions of the United States and Canada (renamed in 1886 the American Federation of Labor) passed a resolution that was sponsored by Gabriel Edmonston of the Carpenters Union. It read as follows:

"RESOLVED . . . that eight hours shall constitute a legal day's labor, from and after May 1, 1886, and that we recommend to labor unions throughout this jurisdiction that they so direct their laws to conform to this resolution by the time named."

Mr. Edmonston may have chosen May 1 as a memorial to those who 17 years earlier had tried to win the eight hour day in Chicago and failed. It may have been that as a carpenter Gabriel Edmonston realized that May 1 was a good time for renewal of contracts and winning shorter hours. The building trades in Chicago and many other parts of the country came alive again after the long winter, and contractors were willing to settle fast to get the men working.

The Knights of Labor, the nation's largest union, and its leader, Terrance Powderly, did not support the "Eight Hour Day Movement." However, in Chicago, the Knights of Labor had members like Albert Parsons, and the Chicago Knights refused to follow Powderly's advice and enthusiastically joined in the fight.

Events began on May Day, 1886 with 340,000 workers in 12,000 factories across the country laying down their tools. Over 80,000 of these workers were in Chicago, testifying to the strength of Chicago as a union town. Before the strike began 45,000 workers in Chicago were promised the eight hour day by their employers.

In what is generally regarded around the world as the first May Day parade, Albert Parsons, his wife Lucy, and their two children Albert Jr. and Lulu led 80,000 workers up Michigan Avenue, singing, arm-in-arm.

Although there were smaller marches on Sunday, May 2, it was the meeting that Spies spoke to near the McCormick Plant on Monday, May 3 and the Haymarket Meeting on Tuesday evening May 4 that attracted the largest crowds of workers.

THE HAYMARKET PROTEST MEETING

Probably no meeting was more poorly planned than the Haymarket Protest Meeting of Tuesday, May 4, 1886. Gottfried Waller, who first proposed the meeting, only stayed for fifteen minutes. Adolph Fischer, who was in charge of publicity, dropped by for a while and then went to the bar on the ground floor of Zepf's Hall for a drink. George Engel, another member of the committee, stayed home to play cards and drink beer with his wife and friends. Engel only heard about the bombing when Waller rushed over to tell him about it.

During and after the Haymarket Trial there were rumors throughout the city that Gottfried Waller was a police agent, hired to stir up trouble. Many believed that this is why he didn't stay at the meeting, and why he served as a state's witness against the others. His rent and expenses during and after the trial were paid by Captain Schaack of the Chicago Avenue Police Station.

Over 20,000 flyers were printed and distributed announcing the meeting which was supposed to start at half past seven. Although over 2,500 people were roaming about by 7:30, no speakers arrived and many left in disgust. It was 8:30 p.m. before August Spies mounted a discarded old wagon parked near Crane's Alley on Desplaines Street, a half a block from Haymarket Square. Spies didn't know what to do; he sent out a messenger to look for Parsons, Fielden, or anyone else who could help him out and say something to the crowd. Therefore, none of those who spoke at the meeting had been instrumental in planning it. Only Spies had had anything even indirectly to do with the meeting; Fielden and Parsons didn't even know a meeting was taking place until fifteen minutes before they spoke.

Despite protests from Captain Bonfield and the Chicago Police Department, Mayor Carter Harrison had issued a permit for the Haymarket meeting. One reason so many people came was because it was a legal gathering sanctioned by the Mayor.

Harrison, a Democrat, had been having trouble controlling the Police Department ever since he was first elected in 1879. Harrison was well liked by the workers of the city, and he had appointed many Socialists to the city administration to the great dismay of the Republican businessmen of Chicago. Despite orders from the Mayor, policemen like Inspector Bonfield and Captain Schaack continued to work openly with the William Pinkerton Detective Agency and the businessmen. In issuing permission for the meeting, Harrison may have wished the exposure of obvious examples of "police brutality" and public criticism of Inspector Bonfield and Capt. Schaack.

Mayor Harrison came to the Haymarket meeting early and stayed almost to the very end. After listening to a short presentation by August Spies, and an hour long presentation by Albert Parsons, the Mayor left the meeting at about 10 p.m. as Samuel Fielden was beginning to speak. Harrison went a half block south to the Desplaines Street Police Station to tell Bonfield and Ward to send their men home, since the meeting was almost over. The Mayor had agreed to stationing 176 policeman at the Desplaines precinct in case of trouble.

Instead of going home right away the Mayor returned to the meeting for a short time and then mounted his white horse to ride west to his nearby mansion on Ashland Avenue. Bonfield had several policemen dressed as workers running back and forth between the police station and the meeting directly to the north. These plainclothesmen reported to Bonfield when the Mayor had left, and then Ward and Bonfield ordered their men to march and disperse the meeting. Mayor Harrison had just undressed and was getting into bed at 10:30 when he heard the explosion of the bomb and heard the shots. It has always been a mystery why Bonfield disobeyed the Mayor and was so anxious to have him out of the way.

Despite what most history books say about 1,000 to 3,000 people being at the meeting when the police attacked, there were actually only about 200 workers left when the 176 policemen under Ward and Bonfield struck. They used a new military formation for crowd control that they had been practicing for months. Many patrons leaving a nearby theatre were also clubbed by the police. Then suddenly the mysterious bomb was thrown by someone unknown to this day.

Today we read about bombings in various parts of the world everyday, but this was the first time such a device was ever used in the United States. The bomb in no way helped the cause of the "Eight Hour Day Movement"; it was in fact used by the businessmen and the newspapers to destroy the struggle for shorter hours and the labor movement as well. Even Carter Harrison was forced the following morning, Wednesday, May 5, to declare "Martial Law" in Chicago and to go along with Bonfield and the business community for several weeks in order not to appear soft on "law and order."

"MAKE THE RAIDS FIRST AND LOOK UP THE LAW AFTERWARDS"

State's Attorney Julius S. Grinnell, who would later prosecute the Haymarket Eight, stated that the police that made the raids beginning on May 5 should disregard the law. Hundreds of workers in Chicago were arrested for no reason. Meeting halls, newspaper offices, and even private homes were broken into without search warrants. Professor Harvey Wish said the following about this terrible period in Chicago history:

"Homes were invaded without a warrant and ransacked for evidence; suspects were beaten and subjected to the 'third degree'; individuals ignorant of the meaning of socialism and anarchism were tortured by the police, sometimes bribed as well, to act as witnesses for the state."

State's Attorney Julius Grinnel

Of the hundreds arrested only 31 were indicted, and this number was finally cut to only eleven. Gottfried Waller and William Seliger were never brought to trial since they agreed to turn state's witnesses. Rudolph Schnaubelt was never found. Therefore only eight were actually tried, and only two of these men were at the Haymarket meeting when the bomb was thrown. The Haymarket Eight were a cross section of the Chicago labor movement of that day. They included a militant preacher, trade union organizers, members of the labor press, and men involved in community and political action.

Newspapers screamed for blood; even the respectable Albany Law Journal for May 15, 1886 would say the following:

[The recent events in Chicago] "have revived very strongly in us several desires long vaguely entertained, such as a check upon immigration, a power of deportation, a better equipment of the police, a prompter and severer dealing with disorder in its first overt act. It is a serious thought that the lives of good and brave men, the safety of innocent women and children, and immunity of property should be, even for one hour, in a great city, at the mercy of a few long-haired, wild-eyed, bad-smelling, atheistic, reckless foreign wretches, who never did an honest hour's work in their lives, but who, driven half crazy with years of oppression and mad with envy of the rich, think to level society and its distinctions with a few bombs. There ought to be some law . . . to enable society to crush such snakes when they raise their heads before they have time to bite . . . This state of things almost justifies the resort to the vigilance committee and lynch law . . . It seems that the penal law of Illinois would warrant treating all these godless fiends as murderers, and we hope they will be so treated and extirpated from the face of the earth."

Churches condemned the anarchists in Sunday sermons for several weeks. They were suspicious of the Knights of Labor as a secret society that pledged the loyalty of its members to worldly problems instead of to the church and spiritual needs. They thought of the anarchists as atheists and against God. The American Protestant churches were involved at this time in two questions . . . the preservation of Sunday as a religious day, and the Prohibition movement. The churches saw the labor movement as opposed to both these issues. The magazine, the Christian Advocate, said the following at this time:

"Sunday traffic, Sunday excursions, Sunday newspapers, noon editions of Sunday papers, Sunday theaters, open saloons on Sunday, and suspected Anarchist meetings at which treason is preached . . . then surprise and whines when the red flag explodes its bomb."

WHO WERE THE SO-CALLED "ANARCHISTS" AND WHAT DID THEY BELIEVE IN?

Americans today have a picture of an anarchist as someone who is against all government and for a social structure without law or order. When we think of an anarchist we think of a sinister, bearded figure throwing a bomb. But where did we get this kind of stereotype?

Our stereotype of an anarchist came from the cartoons that were published in anti-labor newspapers in the United States and around the world. These cartoons appeared during the trial and for years afterwards. But if this was not an accurate representation of their ideas, then what did these men believe in?

Each of the Haymarket Eight believed in different philosophies. They ranged from Oscar Neebe, who was perhaps the most conservative, to Louis Lingg, the youngest and most radical. Most of them had read the writings of Thomas Jefferson and Thomas Paine. Albert Parsons particularly liked a quote of Jefferson's at the time of Shay's Rebellion, when wealthly Massachusetts bankers were foreclosing on the land of small New England farmers, and the farmers rose up to protect their property.

"God forbid we should ever be twenty years without such a rebellion . . . What country can preserve its liberties if its rulers are not warned from time to time that this people preserve the spirit of resistance? Let them take arms. What signify a few lives lost in a century or two? The tree of liberty must be refreshed from time to time by the blood of patriots and tyrants. It is its natural manure."

To most of the Haymarket Eight the word "anarchism" meant "freedom". They saw the government, the businessmen, and the police working in violation of the principles we fought for during the American Revolution. They feared the great new concentration of wealth that had taken place since the Civil War. They were concerned about the new machinery that was replacing even the most skilled workmen.

During the Haymarket Trial Albert Parsons was asked about his philosophy of government, and he said the following:

"I am an Anarchist . . . What is Socialism, or Anarchism? Briefly stated, it is the right of the toilers to the free and equal use of the tools of production and the right of the producers to their product. That is Socialism."

Chicago anarchists, unlike some of the New York anarchists, were really Syndicalists who believed in worker control over key industries. Today in Sweden, Germany, and even England workers are now allowed by law to elect representatives to the Boards of Directors of large companies producing steel, automobiles, and other major consumer items. The Haymarket Eight were far ahead of their time. Chicagoans in the 1880's regarded such ideas as contrary to "property rights" and the "American Way of Life".

Did the Haymarket Eight believe in the use of bombs to level American society? There is no doubt that several of the eight talked about using the new dynamite that had been developed in Sweden by Nobel. But articles from newspapers and quotes of prominent businessmen such as Thomas A. Scott of the Pennsylvania Railroad who talked of using dynamite against workers when they went on strike had been read first by several of the Haymarket Eight; and they were horrified by the attitude of the Chicago Times, Daily News, and Tribune, which talked of using dynamite against starving workers.

The Haymarket Eight saw the cheap, light, new dynamite as a way of protecting a legally assembled group of workers if they were attacked by the police or troops. They saw it as a way of protecting their wives and children if they were being clubbed as they had been during the "Bread Riot" and the Railroad Strike of 1877. They saw the dynamite bomb as a leveler, giving the average worker for the first time a chance to protect himself against the government that was one by one taking away his freedoms under the Constitution. At least seven of the Haymarket Eight did a lot of talking about bombs, but none of them ever used one. If talking about using them was grounds for execution, then many newspaper editors and businessmen should also have been brought to trial.

Only one of the eight actually was proven to have been in the possession of bombs, and that was Louis Lingg, the 21 year old German carpenter who lived with Mr. and Mrs. William Seliger. Lingg had only been in the United States a year, and he only rented space in the Seliger House. The Seligers seemed to have been making bombs long before he arrived. They turned state's witnesses, testified against him, and Lingg was given the death penalty. They received a trip back to Germany where they lived for the rest of their lives.

Although Lingg had helped make a number of bombs with Mr. Seliger, he was several miles away from Haymarket Square when the bomb was thrown. It was never proven positively that the bomb thrown was one that he or Mr. Seliger had made.

THE TRIAL

The trial opened on June 21, 1886 with seven of the Haymarket Eight present. Then Albert Parsons dramatically turned himself in. Although he had been completely safe in Wisconsin, and there is no question but that he could have escaped execution by remaining away until the hysteria had died down, Parsons, stating that he was innocent, freely turned himself in to stand trial with his friends.

The usual method of picking the trial jurors by lot was cast aside in this case, and the trial judge appointed Henry L. Ryce as a special bailiff and gave him personal power to select the prospective jurors. Ryce placed on the juror list only persons of obvious bias against the Haymarket Eight. Later a Chicago businessman, Otis S. Favor, swore under oath that Ryce had said the following to him in the presence of witnesses:

"I am managing this case, and know what I am about. These fellows are going to be hanged as certain as death. I am calling such men as the defendants will have to challenge peremptorily and waste their time and challenges. They then will have to take such men as the prosecution wants."

The Haymarket Eight and their attorneys Captain William Black, Moses Salomen, Sigismund Zeisler, and William A. Foster, hoped to have Judge Tuley, the most liberal of the Chicago judges, as the trial judge, but instead Judge Joseph E. Gary was assigned to the case.

Gary made the trial a travesty of justice. Gary could have seen that the jury was not stacked, but instead he made things worse. Years later he unwittingly condemned his own conduct when he said ". . . . if I had a little strained the law . . . I was to be commended for so doing." Gary ignored the fact that one of the jurors was a relative of one of the policemen that died as a result of the Haymarket bomb. He forced all eight men to be tried together in a "Conspiracy Trial" on the basis that if one was guilty and the others knew each other and had conspired, then all were guilty. This was similar in many ways to the infamous "Chicago Eight Conspiracy Trial" presided over by Judge Julius Hoffman in 1969.

Gary would only allow Captain Black to cross-examine the State's witnesses on specific points brought out by the state. However, the State's Attorney was allowed to drag in any police to display all kinds of bombs and dynamite to scare the jury, and Gary made insulting remarks about the Haymarket Eight throughout the trial. Articles from labor newspapers mentioning bombs were brought in as evidence by the State's Attorney, but Captain Black was not allowed to bring in Tribune articles suggesting the use of bombs against the workers.

The fact that this trial was about ideas and not deeds was stated by the State's Attorney, Grinnel, in his summation to the jury:

"Law is on trial. Anarchy is on trial. These men have been selected, picked out by the grand jury and indicted because they are the leaders. They are no more guilty than the thousands who follow them. Gentlemen of the Jury; convict these men, make examples of them, hang them and you save our institutions, our society."

Inside the Cook County Court House during the Haymarket Trial.

The jury did find them guilty and eventually all but Oscar Neebe were sentenced to die by hanging. Although even the State's Attorney Grinnel had recommended that charges against Neebe be dropped, Judge Gary gave him 15 years at hard labor at Joliet Prison.

Writing about the trial in his book *The Trial of the Judgement*, General Matthew Mark Trumbull, a distinguished northern general during the Civil War said the following about the Haymarket Trial:

"In the trial of the Anarchists the law itself was bent and strained to the breaking point. On the floor of the court-house they stood at a perilous disadvantage. The scales of justice were not poised evenly between the accused and the State. They were poor; the prosecution rich. The whole machinery of the city and county government was at the service of the prosecution. The treasury was reckless of cost. The police force, the detective force, and every official influence were active against the prisoners. They were beaten from the start. In the arena of life or death they fought against odds unfair and invincible. They played for a jury with dice loaded against them. The indictment was a bewildering contradiction of sixty-nine discordant counts, and every count was the horn of a dilemma. The course pursued by the counsel for the State was unfair throughout the trial.

WORLDWIDE PROTEST

It soon became obvious to the trade unionists of both the American Federation of Labor and the Knights of Labor that the Haymarket Trial was more than just a trial of eight men. A partner in a large Chicago clothing firm said what probably was in the minds of many businessmen:

"No, I don't consider these people to have been found guilty of any offense, but they must be hanged . . . I'm not afraid of anarchy; oh, no, it's the utopian scheme of a few a very few philanthropic cranks, who are amiable withal, but I do consider that the labor movement must be crushed! The Knights of Labor will never dare to create discontent again if these men are hanged."

The actual hanging was delayed by an appeal to the Illinois Supreme Court. The appeal was denied on the basis that Socialism was the advocacy of the theft of private property and the jurors had a right to be prejudiced against the defendants who were Socialists. The hanging was then rescheduled for Nov. 11, 1887 for seven of the defendants.

Another appeal was made to the United States Supreme Court by the Honorable Leonard Sweet, an old law associate of Abraham Lincoln, but the appeal was denied nine days before the execution.

All over the United States trade union groups began to sign resolutions and make appeals. The Central Labor Union of New York passed a resolution asking organized labor all over the country to hold giant mass protest meetings. Samuel Gompers got the A.F. of L. to pass a similar resolution and he said: "I am opposed to the execution. It would be a blot on . . . our country." Gompers later said that "Labor must do its best to maintain justice for the radicals or find itself denied the rights of free men."

Not only labor but prominent Americans in all walks of life were changing their minds about the justness of this case. Novelist William Dean Howells, former U.S. Senator and Illinois Supreme Court Judge Lyman Trumbull, Henry Demarest Lloyd the noted writer, the son of John Brown, banker Lyman Gage, and Murray Taley, Chief Justice of the Illinois Circuit Court, were among those who, like Moncure D. Conway, the biographer of Thomas Paine, were saying that this frame-up was "the greatest wrong that ever threatened our fame as a nation." But businessmen like Marshall Field, George Pullman, and Richard Crane continued to hold fast to the idea that they must die.

All over England workers protested. Oscar Wilde circulated a petition, English workers in 49 different cities held rallies, and William Morris and the young George Bernard Shaw addressed a rally on October 22, 1887. Shaw said:

". . . If you think that by hanging us you can stamp out the labor movement . . . the movement from which the downtrodden millions, the millions who toil in want and misery—expect salvation—if this is your opinion, then hang us! Here you will tread upon a spark, but there and there, behind you and in front of you, and everywhere, flames blaze up. It is a subterranean fire. You cannot put it out."

In Germany, Bismarck became so concerned with German workers' reactions to the Haymarket Affair that he banned all public meetings. In France, the French Chamber of Deputies on October 29, 1887 telegraphed the Governor of Illinois protesting the coming execution. The petition called the impending executions a "political crime" which would be an "everlasting mark of infamy upon republicanism." Meetings of workers were also held in Holland, Russia, Italy, and Spain and from all over the world contributions came in to the defense fund.

On November 10, the day before the execution, Samuel Gompers came from Washington to appeal to Governor Oglesby for the last time. The national and worldwide pressures did finally force the Governor to change the sentences of Samuel Fielden and Michael Schwab to imprisonment for life.

Although five of the eight were still to be hung the next day, on the morning of November 10, Louis Lingg was found in his cell, his head half blown away by a dynamite cap. The entire event was most mysterious, since Lingg was hoping to receive a pardon that very day. Why would he kill himself?

Although the explosion took place at 8:55 a.m., the young and very strong man lived until 2:51 p.m. in the afternoon. How he received the cap after he and his cell had been searched, after he had been moved to a lower tier of cells away from the other seven, and had been allowed no visitors, has never been explained.

THE EXECUTION AND THE FUNERAL

The Chicago Police Department and the newspapers feared civil war in Chicago the day that the execution took place. Every available policeman and even members of the National Guard were stationed around the County Court House and Jail. There is no doubt that there were enough workers in the city ready to storm the jail and friends even suggested this idea to Spies, Engel, Parsons, and Fischer. The condemned men made their friends pledge not to carry out any such foolish plans.

The families of the condemned men thought they would be able to see them early in the morning of November 11th, but when they appeared they were either arrested or turned away by the police. At 11:30 a.m. the sheriff went from cell to cell to get each of the condemned men, and by noon they had been hung. Friday, November 11, 1887 became known around the world as "Black Friday."

Messengers carried the news that the execution was over from the jail to especially prepared bulletin boards in the downtown area, to the newspapers, and to the private clubs of the rich. One local merchant said business that day was terrible, but he predicted that now that it was all over and they were dead, business would return to normal in the city.

On the next day, Saturday, November 12, the bodies of the men were returned to their families and friends. Thousands of people went to their homes and filed by their bodies all that day to pay their last respects. Buildings in the ethnic Polish, German, and other working class neighborhoods along Milwaukee Avenue were covered with black bunting.

On Sunday, November 13 the funeral began at noon with thousands of workers marching from home to home to pick up the bodies of each of the martyrs. They began at the home of August Spies who lived the farthest from the city. Then along Milwaukee Avenue with nearly half a million people watching, thousands of workers marched solemnly into the downtown area, to the Grand Central Railroad Station, and then by train to the gravesite in German Waldheim Cemetery ten miles directly west of Chicago in Forest Park, Illinois.

The sun was just setting as the five bodies were placed in the cemetery vault. Thousands of people listened as their attorney, Captain Black, gave the funeral oration. He declared that:

"We do not stand here by the bodies of felons. There is nothing disgraceful about their death. They died for liberty, for the sacred right of untrammeled speech and for humanity. We are proud to have been their friends . . ."

Former United States Senator Lyman Trumball, who narrowly missed being the Republican choice for President in 1860, had this to say about the trial and the execution:

"The time will come when mankind will look back upon the execution of the anarchists as we of this day look back upon the burning of the witches in New England."

GOVERNOR ALTGELD'S PARDON

After the execution the public hysteria that had been promoted by the police and the press began to give way to calmer thinking. The Chicago Times in January of 1889 began a series of stories on police corruption and Inspector Bonfield and Captain Schaack of the Chicago Avenue Police Station were found to be the leaders. They were receiving payments from gamblers, prostitutes, and petty thieves to allow them to continue unmolested while they were collecting money from the businessmen to set up "The Red Squad" to infiltrate unions and other community organizations.

Inspector Bonfield ordered the arrest of the editors of the Chicago Times and tried to shut down that newspaper just as he had earlier done to the labor press. This was too much for the public, and both Schaack and Bonfield were forced to resign.

When the business community cut off its contributions to the police department for "The Red Squad", the police suddenly made more raids and spread more stories of anarchist revolts. Judge Tuley, whom the Haymarket Eight had wanted for their judge instead of Judge Gary, said the following in early 1889:

"The Anarchists have the same rights as other citizens to assemble peaceably for the discussion of their views; . . . the police have no right to presume an intention on their part to break the laws; . . . their meetings must not be prohibited or interfered with until a breach of the law is actually committed; . . . in no other city of the United States except Chicago have the police officials attempted to prevent the right of free speech on such unwarranted pretences and assumptions of power, and . . . it is time to call a halt."

Clarence Darrow, then a young partner in the law firm of John Peter Altgeld, and George Schilling, a political advisor to Altgeld and a friend of several of the Haymarket Martyrs, had tried for a long time to get Altgeld to take a stand on the Haymarket case. Altgeld had refused but when he was elected governor in November of 1892, many of his supporters felt he would pardon Neebe, Schwab, and Fielden as soon as he took office. Altgeld hesitated to act but he was secretly reading the transcripts of the case and sending Schilling out to get sworn statements from many who were involved in the case.

With public opinion changing, Judge Gary found himself being seriously criticized all over the country. Even the

Chicago Bar Association censured his behavior and eventually he was removed from the bench. In order to fight such criticism Gary wrote an article for Century magazine in April of 1893 stating that "the anarchists were rightly punished, not for opinions, but for horrible deeds." The judge went on to attack the motives of the defense attorney in the case, and he issued a blanket attack on unions, stating that they were agents of violence and revolution.

Judge Joseph Gary

As a result of Judge Gary's article the public was again talking about Haymarket, and more people were asking for the release of the three men from Joliet Prison. Clarence Darrow thought it would be good politically for Altgeld to pardon the men at this time. But Altgeld said: "If I conclude to pardon those men, it will not meet with the approval you expect . . . From that day, I will be a dead man!"

No one knew what Altgeld would do although a speech before the graduating class of the University of Illinois on June 7, 1893 did provide a clue. On that occasion he said:

"You turn to the courts of justice; . . . and you say . . . here wrongs are corrected, the strong are curbed, and the weak protected. You will be disappointed. The administration of justice, or rather of laws . . . is only a struggling toward the right . . . The men who administer the laws are human, with all the failings of humanity. They take their biases, their prejudices with them on to the bench. Upon the whole, they try to do the best they can; but the wrongs done in the courts of justice themselves are so great that they cry to heaven . . ."

On June 25, 1893 a beautiful monument to the Haymarket Martyrs was dedicated in Waldheim Cemetery with 8,000 people present, many of them foreign visitors attending the Chicago Columbian Exposition. Delegations from Belgium, France, and England placed flowers on the monument and many newspaper stories were written about this event. Governor Altgeld decided to take this opportunity to announce his decision to pardon Neebe, Schwab, and Fielden.

On June 26, Altgeld signed the papers granting the pardon. Mr. E. S. Dreyer, a banker who served as foreman of the grand jury which had originally indicted the men, had changed his mind about their guilt and decided to devote the rest of his life to getting the remaining three released from jail. He was present when the governor signed the pardon and he begged Altgeld to allow him to take the pardons personally to Joliet Prison. Dreyer caught the train from Springfield to Joliet with the pardon in the morning, and by mid-afternoon, unashamedly weeping, Dreyer presented the pardons to the men and escorted them back to Chicago where they were jubilantly welcomed despite their pleas that they wanted to return quietly to their homes and families.

Nevertheless Altgeld was correct about the general public reaction to the pardon. Cartoonists depicted him as an anarchist. The newspapers emphasized Altgeld's German ancestry, depicting him as being un-American. The Chicago Tribune led the attack with these words:

"The anarchists believed that he (Altgeld) was not merely an alien by birth, but an alien by temperament and sympathies, and they were right. He has apparently not a drop of true American blood in his veins. He does not reason like an American, not feel like one, and consequently does not behave like one."

The Pullman Strike followed a year later and Altgeld again took the side of the workers. Haymarket and Pullman together brought about his defeat in the election of 1896. The bankers and businessmen who disagreed with his actions demanded immediate payment on all his debts, almost bankrupting him. His former partner Clarence Darrow eventually came to his aid and saved him by making him a partner in his firm. In 1902, while protesting against the British treatment of the Boers in Africa, Altgeld had a stroke on the stage of the Joliet Opera House. He died within hours.

Over 150,000 people filed by his body while it was on display in the Randolph Street entrance of the Chicago Public Library, and Jane Addams, William Jennings Bryan, and Clarence Darrow all eulogized him as a man who always remained true to the workers of Illinois.

THE SIGNIFICANCE OF HAYMARKET IN THE YEARS SINCE 1886 AND TODAY

The Haymarket bomb, the May Day march for the eight hour day, the trial, and execution started a chain of events that have influenced every corner of the globe.

The American Federation of Labor refused to give up the "Eight Hour Day Movement" even though public hysteria had weakened the labor movement and resulted in the loss of the shorter work day even in shops where it had been won earlier. At the A.F. of L. Convention in St. Louis in December of 1888, the day of May 1, 1890 was officially set aside for the renewal of the movement. The watchwords for the struggle would be "Eight Hours, Firm Peaceable and Positive", and the slogan was again "Eight hours for work, Eight hours for rest, Eight hours for what we will".

In July of 1889, Samuel Gompers and the American Federation of Labor managed to scrape enough money together to send a delegate to the International Labor Congress in Paris which was set for the hundredth anniversary of the beginning of the French Revolution, Bastile Day, July 14, 1889. At this time the A.F. of L. delegate, Hugh McGregor asked that the International Labor Congress adopt May Day as an International Labor Day. Workers would march on this day for the eight hour day, democracy, and the rights of workers to organize. This day would also be a memorial to the "Martyrs of Chicago". Later, at an international socialist conference in Geneva, Switzerland in 1892, a delegate from the Knights of Labor made a similar resolution and it was adopted.

Even Peter J. McGuire, who is known as the "Father of Labor Day" (the first Monday in September) began to favor having May Day adopted throughout the world. In America, McGuire's union, the Carpenters and Joiners, gained dramatically in membership as a result of the solidarity of the May Day marches for shorter hours. Louis Lingg had been a member of their union.

In 1894, Grover Cleveland suddenly announced that the first Monday in September would be Labor Day in America, and he signed a bill to make this a national holiday. Peter McGuire and other trade unions had been lobbying for this bill since 1882, and now, perhaps as a way of calming the American labor movement's enthusiasm for May Day, Cleveland gave in to the September date. Beginning in the 1950's the American Bar Association sought to have May Day referred to as "Law Day" in the United States.

Today only Canada and the United States use the September date, while the rest of the world uses May Day as the workers' day. French Canadians have rebelled against the September day in the last few years and have begun to use May Day. In recent years it has become increasingly evident that the September date is not a purely union workers' day, but also a holiday for businessmen, bankers, lawyers, and stockbrockers. During the Nixon Administration the significance of Labor Day became "productivity" and the "gospel of work" instead of the contributions of the American labor movement to our society.

The Haymarket bomb, the trial and execution, and the sudden interest in a world-wide celebration of May Day, all these things were to have a profound effect on the city of Chicago.

Many members of the Union League Club in Chicago were horrified by the growth of labor unions and the Haymarket bomb. Sidney Corning Eastman, a prominent attorney, after walking along the lake front and listening to one of the rallies of the workers, issued an "Open Letter to the Union League Club". This open letter was eventually printed up as a 21 page pamphlet that was distributed to all members of the club. It stated that because of all these foreign groups in Chicago and their agitation, we must have a revival of American Patriotism. Members of the club felt that these foreigners *must* follow the American way and who personified that more than George Washington? Pullman, Marshall Field, and other members agreed to lobby for the annual celebration of Washington's Birthday. They said that to perpetuate "the ideals of loyalty which were personified in Washington by an annual tribute to his character as a man and his service as a military leader and president" would exercise an elevating influence upon the life of the community.

It is ironic that the labor movement struck back by deciding to use Washington's Birthday in 1889 as a kick-off to their new "Eight Hour Day Movement" set for May, 1890. But the businessmen of Chicago wanted more than just Washington's Birthday; they wanted military protection as a check on labor agitation in the city. Marshall Field, who was a member of both the Commercial Club and the Union League Club, rose before the Commercial Club and made one of his rare speeches. Field argued that there should be a regiment of soldiers nearer Chicago "instead of a thousand miles away, like Fort Laramie or Fort Riley".

John Farwell, another prominent Chicagoan, explained the need for the fort proposed by Marshall Field by saying that "the theory was that if they had some troops nearby, it would act as a preventive and prevent a lot of riots occurring in Chicago because the soldiers could get there so quickly."

With both Field and John V. Farwell in back of such a proposal, the Commercial Club and many members of the Union League Club personally raised money to buy 632 acres of ground thirty miles north of Chicago at Highland, Illinois. In October of 1887 the land was presented to the United States Army with the understanding that troops would be permanently stationed here. The fort was soon expanded to 725 acres and named Ft. Highland until the death of General Sheridan, who had been a close friend of Marshall Field and George Pullman. The fort was then renamed Fort Sheridan and it took as its motto the phrase "Essential to Freedom since 1887".

Later, a military highway, Sheridan Road, would connect the fort to the city so that troops could be moved quickly from the fort to Chicago. Armories were later built in ethnic industrial neighborhoods to house the troops during times of strikes and demonstrations. Many of the rich members of the Union League Club and the Commerical Club built palatial mansions along the North Shore near Fort Sheridan, leaving their older mansions along Rush Street, Prairie Avenue, and Ashland Avenue. Never again would they have to live in fear as they had during the Railroad Strike of 1877. Never again could someone like Albert and Lucy Parsons lead a "Poor Peoples March" up their street demanding food and jobs as they had on Thanksgiving Day 1884.

Not to be outdone by the Union League Club and the Commercial Club, the smaller Merchants' Club gave 100 acres to the United States Navy, for the establishment of a naval base near Chicago. The Great Lakes Naval Station base, although 800 miles from salt water, would become the largest training base for sailors in the world. With the addition of this base Chicago was protected by water as well as by land.

On the world scene the observance of May Day grew beyond simply being a memorial day for the Haymarket Martyrs. Since May Day many times fell on a work day, it had been understood that the nearest Sunday would be used as the day of observance if marching on the work day would incite police and troop action against the workers.

On May Day, 1905, a work day, Russian workers in St. Petersburg gathered around the Royal Palace in hopes of having their representatives talk with the Czar and protest against the starvation resulting from the Russo-Japanese War which was still in progress. Instead of talking with the people, Russian troops swept down on the men, women, and children in the crowd killing hundreds of them. This would make May Day not just a memorial for the "Martyrs of Chicago" but one for the murdered workers of St. Petersburg as well.

In 1912, the Industrial Workers of the World tried an "Eight Hour Action" on May Day. Thousands of flyers and stickers were printed throughout the United States and Canada with these words: "I Won't Work more than 8 hours after May 1, 1912. How about you?"

In 1925, in the town of Matehuala, on the main highway between Monterrey and Mexico City, Mexico, the trade unions of the area unveiled in the Plaza de Chicago a monument to the "Martyrs of Chicago". The names of the Haymarket Eight are inscribed on the eight sides of the monument. Each May Day workers from all the surrounding towns come here on the "Day of the Martyrs of Chicago" which is what May Day is called in Mexico.

An outstanding mural by Diego Rivera on the left side of the main staircase in the Palace of Justice in Mexico City shows the Haymarket scene, the trial, and execution, and the faces of the eight men. A beautiful stained glass window in Italy shows the police shooting at the workers with the words McCormick Reaper Company and Haymarket in the distance and a reproduction of the flyer announcing the meeting.

Bismarck outlawed May Day, but German workers fought for years for the right to march on that day. In order to gain support from the labor unions of Germany in 1933, Adolph Hitler gave in to the demand of German workers for the right to march on May Day. After allowing the workers to march on May 1, 1933, he signed legislation on May 2 outlawing the free trade union movement in Germany.

Although Americans have generally observed the first Monday in September as Labor Day, during the depression years of the 1930's there was a revival of interest in May Day. In Chicago, Lucy Parsons marched with her young friend Studs Terkel and many labor groups, until her death in 1942.

With the coming of the Vietnam War, the Civil Rights Marches of the 1960's, police brutality during the Democratic Convention in Chicago in 1968, the "Chicago Eight Conspiracy Trial" and Watergate, many people began to look again at the "Haymarket Affair" and what it should have taught us.

The Police Monument in Haymarket Square again became a symbol of "police brutality" as described in the Walker Report and the Kerner Report. The statue was bombed twice and finally had to be guarded twenty-four hours a day and eventually moved.

In 1975, the Chicago "Red Squad" again made news when it was discovered that they were using federal law enforcement funds to spy on innocent people and to infiltrate community organizations in Chicago that were trying to bring about social change. History seemed to be repeating itself.

I do not believe it is an overstatement to say that probably no event has had such a profound influence on the American labor movement or on the history of Chicago than what happened near Haymarket Square in 1886. Through the association of the "Haymarket Affair" and May Day the impact has been worldwide. Revolutions have taken place and many peoples lives have been changed by the events that began on Saturday, May 1, 1886. All of the labor, political, and community leaders buried in Waldheim Cemetery wished to be buried there because they said that the Haymarket Affair, the trial, and execution were a turning point in their lives.

Today with unemployment increasing, automation leaving more and more workers unemployed, with workers now demanding a "Six Hour Day", labor and community groups again see the necessity for political and social change. The things that Albert Parsons, August Spies, and the others were saying in 1886 are as pertinent today as they were then. How will America and Americans react to these new cries for change?

I hope by revisiting the sites connected with Haymarket you will see the tragedy of this event and the mistakes that were made by American society at that time. I hope you will see how difficult the struggle for economic security and democracy on the job has been for the American worker. But above all I would hope that "Haymarket Revisited" will make you realize that the struggle is far from won. The battle for social justice, freedom of speech and assembly and democracy in the work place that the Haymarket Martyrs fought is still the battle today.

William J. Adelman

Associate Professor of Labor and Industrial Relations at the University of Illinois, and Vice President of the Illinois Labor History Society.

HAYMARKET REVISITED

Note: Before starting these tours, be sure to read the Introduction for an overview of the significance of the Haymarket Affair. The Introduction will also get you in the mood to better appreciate your tour as you travel on the same streets and by the same buildings that the Haymarket Martyrs knew. Perhaps you might wish to read Henry David's definitive book, *The History of the Haymarket Affair*, or some of the other books on Haymarket from the Reading List at the back of this book.

The Time Line section of this guide will help you to check the chronological order of the events leading up to the Haymarket Affair as well as the many things that have happened since. The tours will be more enjoyable if two or more people go together with one driving and the others reading aloud from the guide. Since city traffic is difficult during the week, a Saturday or Sunday is the best time to take your tour. You will certainly not wish to take the entire tour in one day, therefore it has been broken into four smaller tours. The time it would take to visit all 124 sites is approximately six hours.

TOUR I—will take you to Haymarket Square and the sites connected with the protest meeting and the mysterious bombing. In Haymarket Square you will sense how Chicago workers must have felt in 1886 toward the power structure of the city that refused to help them or understand their problems. The touring time from site 1 to 17 will take you approximately one hour.

TOUR II—will take you to the site of the Haymarket trial and the execution. This trial was one of the most unjust in the history of American jurisprudence. You will see what a circus the trial became and you will sense the tragedy of the Haymarket Eight and their families as the moment of the execution came. The touring time from sites 18 to 29 will take about one hour.

TOUR III—Takes you through many of the ethnic neighborhoods of Chicago . . . German, Polish, Serbian, Russian, Ukranian, Italian, and Jewish. It was here the Haymarket Martyrs and the workers of Chicago lived. These neighborhoods are still the homes of many of the same groups as well as more recently arrived groups of Mexicans, Puerto Ricans, and Blacks. Rich ethnic businessmen also lived in Wicker Park and along Milwaukee because they were not allowed to live on Chicago's Gold Coast with the rich Anglo-Saxon Protestants. You will see the great mansions they built in order to show off their newly acquired wealth. You will also retrace the route of the Haymarket Martyrs' Funeral held Sunday, November 13, 1887 two days after the execution. It was witnessed by over half a million people. The touring time for sites 30 to 89 is about two and a half hours.

TOUR IV—will take you to German Waldheim Cemetery (now Forest Home) where the martyrs are buried. A beautiful monument marks the site there. In Waldheim you will also find "Dissenters' Row", the graves of twenty-four people whose lives were changed and inspired by the Haymarket Affair. These people worked in many different ways for social justice, civil rights, freedom of speech and assembly, and a better life for all Americans. The cemetery is opened during the summer from 8 a.m. to 8 p.m., and during the winter the hours are from 8 a.m. to dusk. The cemetery offices are open from 10 a.m. to 4 p.m. and you may wish to call 366-1900 to make sure the gates will be opened before you drive out. The touring time for sites 90 to 124 (assuming you are coming from downtown Chicago) is about one and a half hours.

1. HAYMARKET SQUARE (Randolph and Desplaines)

NOTE: Park on Randolph, a one-way street going west.

Haymarket Square in 1886 was one of five market areas in Chicago. Today it is hard to imagine how busy it once was. Market areas like this one were once gathering places for the poor workers of the city, who came here to purchase food directly from the farmers at the lowest possible prices.

In her book, "So Big," Edna Ferber described this square as it once was: *"They turned into Haymarket. It was a tangle of horses, carts, men. The wagons were streaming in from the German truck farms that lay to the north of Chicago as well as from the Dutch farms that lay to the southwest . . . Fruits and vegetables . . . tons of it . . . acres of it . . . piled in wagons that blocked the historic square. An unarmed army bringing food to feed a great city . . ."*

Haymarket Square shortly after the erection of the Police Statue (Courtesy Chicago Historical Society)

Gradually these market areas have been closed down, and today there is no farmers' market in Chicago (See No. 18 for reasons).

Haymarket Square was chosen for the May 4th protest meeting over the other market areas because it could hold 20,000 people, and it was near the north, northwest, and west side worker neighborhoods. There had been some discussion at Grief's Hall on May 3rd about using the Market Square (See No. 15), since the Washington Street Tunnel (See No. 14) would provide protection for the women and children, if the police attacked the meeting. But such an attack by the police was dismissed as unlikely, and they settled on the Haymarket.

A streetcar line once ran down the middle of Randolph Street, and the cars would be blocked by large numbers of people massing in the square. When August Spies arrived shortly after 8:00 p.m. and found about 2,500 wandering about, he directed the audience out of the square to Desplaines Street by Crane's Alley. Spies was afraid that blockage of the streetcars might be used by the police as an excuse to disperse the crowd. Therefore, the so-called "Haymarket Square Riot" didn't even happen in Haymarket Square.

The Haymarket meeting was to start at 7:30 p.m., but it was so badly planned that no speakers appeared until Spies arrived. Spies purposely came late since he was to speak in German, and foreign language speakers were always last.

Spies decided to make the best of a bad situation and organize the meeting himself. He heard someone say they had seen Parsons at the corner of Halsted and Randolph, but by the time he got to the corner Parsons had left. Spies had a friend walk over to the offices on Wells Street of the Arbeiter-Zeitung and Alarm, and he asked Balthasar Rav to look for additional speakers.

Spies mounted a wagon by Crane's Alley and spoke from 8:30 to 9 P.M., when Parsons and Fielden arrived to relieve him. They had quickly walked over from the Alarm office when they got Spies' message calling for help.

Parsons spoke for about one hour and finished about 10 p.m.; then Samuel Fielden spoke. Fielden, was just closing his speech (about 10:25) when 176 policemen marched up the street pushing the 200 people still remaining before them. Almost at once the mysterious bomb was thrown.

2. VESTIBULE-ASSUMED SITE OF BOMB THROWING
(Northeast Corner of Randolph and Desplaines)

When the 176 policemen marched from the Desplaines Street Police Station, they marched in columns from sidewalk to sidewalk, forcing the crowd to scatter. According to Parsons most of the audience was standing south of Crane's Alley until the arrival of the police. After the police arrival, the workers were north of the alley and the police to the south.

If the bomb had been thrown from the sidewalk on the east side of Desplaines from 10 or 15 feet south of Crane's Alley, why didn't a policeman see the bomb thrower? Sixteen witnesses including three policemen and two newspaper reporters saw the bomb in the air south of the alley, but they didn't see who threw it.

According to Ernest Zeisler, the son of one of the Haymarket Trial attorneys, the bomb may have been thrown from this vestibule. If the bomb had been thrown from here, after the columns of the police had passed, then the bomb thrower could have walked eastward on Randolph and escaped into the darkness in all the confusion.

The bomb thrower may have been Rudolph Schnaubelt, who was the brother-in-law of Michael Schwab. Frank Harris in his book, "The Bomb," believed that Schnaubelt was an agent of the police and businessmen and paid to throw it. Albert Parsons also believed that someone had been hired to throw the bomb. If this was the case, the bomb was probably meant to land among the workers, but the police had pushed them north of the alley too quickly.

It seems strange that although Schnaubelt was arrested twice, both times calls came through from City Hall and he was released. Later Schnaubelt made his way to Canada and Europe, settling in Sweden. Frank Harris had Schnaubelt die in Europe, but Lucy Parsons claimed he was still alive in California in the early 1920's. There are many theories about the bombing, but we will probably never know the answer.

As you stand in this vestibule and look in a northwesterly direction to Site No. 7 where the bomb landed, you may wonder if someone could have thrown the bomb this far. However, Schnaubelt was 6 feet 3 inches tall and 225 pounds, while the bomb only weighed about five pounds. Schnaubelt could easily have thrown the bomb the 92 feet from the vestibule to the spot opposite Crane's Alley where it landed near the front column of the police.

3. CRANE'S ALLEY (Eastside of Desplaines, midway between Lake and Randolph)

Crane's Alley has changed a great deal since 1886. It was once closed off at the end and to the north by the huge factory buildings of the Crane Plumbing Co. Most of these buildings were torn down in the 1960's. Today the only original building remaining on this block of Desplaines is the building south of the alley that contains the vestibule mentioned in Site No. 2.

The small store (now boarded over) to the south of the alley had a gas light in front of it in 1886. This gas light provided the only light on the street to illuminate the speakers.

Only one witness, Harry Gilmer, stated that the bomb had been thrown from out of the alley, and he said he had seen Fielden, Fischer, and others lighting the fuse and plotting the bombing. This witness, however, was challenged by sixteen others who swore the bomb was not thrown from the alley and dozens who had seen Fielden on the speakers' wagon and Fischer at Zepf's Hall. This witness, Harry Gilmer, was completely discredited and later turned out to be an agent of the police paid to infiltrate labor and community organizations.

4. SPEAKERS' WAGON AND CRANE FACTORY

The speakers' wagon was parked just 6 to 8 feet north of Cranes' Alley and it was from here that Spies, Parsons, and Fielden spoke. A second wagon was parked 15 to 20 feet further north of the speakers' wagon. Lucy Parsons, Lizzie Holmes, and the Parsons' children, Albert Jr. and Lulu, were seated in the second wagon along with several other women.

August Spies first mounted the wagon at 8:30 along with his brother Henry and began to speak. Spies spotted Parsons in the audience about 9:00 and turned the meeting over to him.

Here is what happened according to the official record of the trial: *"Mayor Harrison, who heard Parsons' speech and attended the meeting for the purpose of dispersing it if anything should occur to require interference, left the meeting at the end of that speech and told Capt. Bonfield, at the station, that 'nothing had occurred yet, or looked likely to occur, to require interference, and that he had better issue orders to his reserves at the other stations to go home,' whereupon Harrison himself went home.*

After Mr. Parsons, Mr. Fielden spoke twenty minutes. After Mr. Fielden had been speaking some ten minutes it is admitted by all the witnesses that a cloud, accompanied by a cold wind, swept over the northern sky, and thereupon Parsons interrupted Fielden, suggesting an adjournment of the meeting to Zepf's hall, a building situated at the northeast corner of Lake and

> *Desplaines streets and a block north from the Haymarket meeting. To this somebody in the audience replied that the hall was occupied by a meeting of the Furniture Workers' Union, and thereupon Fielden suggested that he would be through in a few minutes and then they would go home.*
>
> *This evidence is established by witnesses for the State and the defense.*
>
> *About one-half of the audience dispersed upon Mr. Parsons' motion and Mr. Fielden's suggestion. Mr. Parsons got down from the wagon and went a few feet north, where his family and Mrs. Holmes were seated, assisted them down, and they went together to Zepf's Hall, and were there when the bomb exploded."*

When the police led by Captain Bonfield and Captain Ward arrived at the wagon at about 10:30, Captain Ward demanded that the crowd disperse. Samuel Fielden was just descending from the wagon, saying that it was a peaceful meeting, when the bomb landed directly across the street.

The Crane Factory was one of the largest in Chicago in 1886, and it was rather ironic that the wagon used for the speeches was on this site. The company owner, R. T. Crane was opposed to the eight-hour day, and his company had experienced a number of serious strikes in the early 1880's. R. T. Crane later headed the committee that raised the money for the erection of the Police Statue (Site No. 8). Crane would also bring in foreign workers as strikebreakers, many of these workers coming from Russia and the Ukraine (See Site 64). When Crane died he was buried near George Pullman in a Greek Temple in Graceland Cemetery (Irving and Clark).

The Chicago Landmarks Commission has recommended a monument be erected in this area. The Illinois Labor History Society recommends that the former Crane Factory site (now used to store pipes) become a small park, which could be an ideal location for a monument to freedom of speech and assembly and the struggle for the eight hour day.

5. ZEPF'S HALL (Northeast Corner of Lake and Desplaines)

Zepf's Hall is still standing and in excellent condition at 630 W. Lake Street. Now the Grand Stage Lighting Company, this hall was the meeting place of the Lumbershovers' Union, whose members worked in the lumberyards that lined the banks of the Chicago River. It was this union that had asked Spies to address their striking members at their rally near the McCormick Reaper Plant on May 3.

Because of the rain Albert Parsons, Lucy, and the children with their friend Lizzie Holmes walked over to the Zepf's Tavern, located on the corner of the ground floor of the Hall. They arrived here about 10 to 15 minutes before the bomb was thrown. Parsons met Fischer inside and they all had a drink. Lizzie Holmes described the scene:

"When the noise of the explosion broke on the air Mr. Parsons was standing near the window of Zepf's saloon looking out; Mrs. Parsons and I sat not far away. Fischer, with other comrades, was in the room. Parsons came up to us and said: 'Don't be frightened! Don't be frightened!

'What is it?' I asked, as a perfect hailstorm of bullets rattled about our ears. 'I do not know: maybe the Illinois regiments have brought up their Gatling gun'.

Zepf's Hall as it looked in 1886

Bullets whistled past us through the open door. Fugitives came running in, and everyone started for a room in the back end of the building. Some one shut the door and for some time a number of us were shut up in total darkness, ignorant of what had happened or what our danger was. Presently the door was opened, and one after another we came out and stepped into the street. Everything seemed quiet; from where we stood no excitement could be noticed, no policemen were in sight."

Although the so-called "Riot" lasted only a few minutes, they remained in the hall about 20 minutes. Albert borrowed five dollars from a friend and went to stay at the Holmes house in Geneva, Illinois. Lucy returned home. (For more details on their actions after the bombing see Site No. 81)

Today the meetinghall on the third floor of Zepf's Hall is still intact. This is one of the last old union meeting halls in Chicago.

The Illinois Labor History Society hopes to preserve and restore this historic building and perhaps turn it into a labor history museum at some future date.

6. FORMER SITE OF GRIEF'S HALL (Near corner of Lake and Clinton)

Nothing remains of this site, since the Northwestern Railroad track and station buildings have replaced much of this area. A few old factory building still stand on the southside of Lake Street and an old fire house is in the middle of the northside of the street; but Grief's Hall is gone.

Grief's Hall where the Haymarket Meeting was planned.

Grief's was probably the most popular meeting hall for unions in the 1880's. The hall was so busy on the evening of Monday, May 3 that the group planning the Haymarket Meeting had to meet in the basement.

Gottfried Waller made the suggestion for the meeting. Engel was present at the Monday night meeting, but he never went to the rally the next night. Lingg was drinking upstairs, but never went to the basement. Fischer was asked by Waller to take care of the printing of the flyers.

The police later called this the "Monday Night Conspiracy Meeting" and throughout the trial the police claimed that this meeting planned Haymarket as the beginning of a takeover of Chicago by Communists, anarchists, and subversives.

7. SPOT WHERE THE BOMB LANDED (West side of Desplaines, opposite Crane's Alley)

One policeman, Mathias Degan, was immediately killed by the bomb blast. Officer Hanson lost a leg and John Tyrrell got 8 pieces of the bomb in his leg. Some of the other policemen killed and wounded were probably killed by their own men who fired in all directions in the dark and confusion.

There were reports that some police ran and hid in nearby houses, but Wirt Dexter, the attorney for the leading businessmen of the city, said the following:

"How noble was their conduct! Instead of fleeing and running, they said: 'Fall in, boys,' and the city was saved".

Although history textbooks point out that seven policemen were killed in Haymarket, they fail to mention the workers that were killed and wounded.

The dead included Mathias Lewis, a German shoemaker, 37 years old. He died three days later *"from internal hemorrhaging caused by a pistol ball wound in the right side, said ball being fired by an unknown person during the progress of a riot . . ."*

Another who died was Charles Schumacker, a 19 year-old tailor, who died on May 11 "from shock and hemorrhaging caused by a pistol ball wound fired from a revolver in the hand of some person unknown to the jury."

Two others whose deaths have been verified by death certificates were Carl Kiester, a laborer, and Emil Lutz, a shoemaker.

About twenty-two others were wounded including August Spies' brother, Henry, and Samuel Fielden who was hit in the knee.

Police sketch of the Haymarket Meeting as the bomb exploded. The building in the center of the picture is still standing.

Many bystanders were injured. Robert Schultz, a waiter was coming out of the Lyceum Theatre down the street when he was shot.

Peter Ley was shot in the back, and Mr. B. LePlant of Earl Park, Indiana, who was visiting Chicago said the following:

"I bought some peanuts and was eating them when the bomb went off. . . then a shot broke my leg and I fell. Then a second shot went into my shoulder and a policeman kicked me."

People were dragged into local drug stores for treatment, and many never reported their injuries because they feared arrest by the police.

8. THE POLICE MONUMENT (Northeast corner of Randolph and the Kennedy Expressway)

Although Governor Altgeld and Chicago's Mayor Carter Harrison would both criticize the police department for marching against the workers, the Chicago Tribune began a campaign to erect a statue to glorify the police action. A committee of Chicago businessmen headed by R. T. Crane with publicity from the Tribune would raise over $10,000. The Commercial Club and the Union League Club, as well as businessmen from Aurora, Elgin, and Rockford who opposed unions and the eight hour day, contributed to the fund.

The winning design for the statue was submitted by Charles F. Batcheider of St. Paul, Minnesota, a newspaper reporter, who suggested a policeman with his arm raised. The selection of the winning design took place at the Union League Club on Sept. 25, 1888.

John Gelert was selected as the sculptor to execute the Batcheider design.

Leaving the Union League Club, Gelert observed a policeman named Thomas F. Birmingham, directing traffic at the corner of Clark and Madison. Gelert selected this big Irish cop to be his model, but when the "Committee of Twenty-Five" headed by Crane observed the clay model, they were horrified that the statue looked Irish. They wished a Protestant, Anglo-Saxon looking policeman. Gelert refused to change the figure, but he also used other models since Birmingham was often drunk and unable to pose.

The statue was finally dedicated on Memorial Day, 1889 with about 2,000 people present. It was a rainy spring day and 176 policemen took part in the ceremony, the same number that had marched up Desplaines Street three years earlier. The seventeen year-old son of Mathias Degan unveiled the statue, and Mayor Cregier spoke the following words:

"May it stand here unblemished so long as the metropolis shall endure to say to the millions who come upon it: This is a free and lawful country with plenty of room for the people of all the earth who choose to come here to breathe the free air and to obey these laws, but not an inch of room or an hour to dwell here for those who come for any other purpose."

In the years to come the police statue and Thomas F. Birmingham would both have many problems. Birmingham was paraded around the Columbian Exposition of 1893 as the symbol of the perfect policeman, but in 1898, and again in 1899, Birmingham was brought before the Civil Service Commission for violation of Rules 58, 67, and 73, which meant that Birmingham had been working with criminals and selling stolen merchandise for his own gain. Eventually Birmingham was thrown off the police force and, according to Emma Goldman's book "My Life," died in County Hospital in 1912 after having been a drunk and petty thief on Skid Row for several years.

The statue also encountered its share of problems. In May of 1903 the crest of the City and State were stolen from the base. In the 1920's, a streetcar driver named O'Neil drove his streetcar full speed and jumped the track, knocking it off the base, because he said he was sick of seeing that policeman with his arm raised.

In 1928, the statue was repaired and moved to Union Park about one mile west. In 1956 the statue was moved to a special platform built for it during construction of the Kennedy Expressway. The Haymarket Businessmen's Association sponsored the moving of the statue, hoping it would promote tourists.

On May 4, 1968 the statue was defaced with black paint after an incident in the Civic Center with the police during a demonstration against the Vietnam War.

On Oct. 6, 1969, the statue was blown up, supposedly by the Weatherman Faction of the SDS. Mayor Daley promised to replace it, and Wally Phillips, a disc jockey, helped raise the money. Sculptor Mario Spampinato was hired to restore Gelert's statue. The new statue was unveiled May 4, 1970.

The statue was again blown up on Oct. 6, 1970, and again Spaninato restored it. There was talk of putting a plastic dome over it or making many statues out of fiberglass and replacing them as each new one was blown up, but Mayor Daley wished it restored in the original material. The Mayor ordered round-the-clock security that cost the city $67,440 a year.

In February, 1972 the statue was removed from its base and placed in the lobby of the Central Police Headquarters at State and 11th Streets, a suggestion made earlier by the Illinois Labor History Society in a letter to Mayor Daley.

The base of the statue has not been removed and on it are inscribed the words supposedly spoken by Capt. Ward as he told Fielden to end the meeting. The names of the policemen who died are also listed.

The back of the monument is most ridiculous in light of the true history of the event. The words on the back are "Dedicated by Chicago . . . to her Defenders in the riot of May 4, 1886."

9. FORMER SITE OF STATE HISTORICAL SOCIETY MARKER (Southwest corner of Randolph and Desplaines—Catholic Charities Building)

The Illinois Labor History Society recommended to the Illinois State Historical Society in 1969 that Haymarket Square be declared a State Historical Landmark. Professors Kogan and Adelman of the University of Illinois prepared the wording for a plaque to be placed in the square, but the only site available was the corner of the Catholic Charities Building, since the City of Chicago would not at that time approve a spot.

The plaque was unveiled on May 3, 1970, as hundreds marched around Haymarket singing, and a wreath of red roses was laid below the plaque. Red roses had been carried by the mourners at the original funeral in 1887.

The entire ceremony was filmed by the "Red Squad" of the Chicago Police Department, since disbanded after an investigation in 1975. On the next day, May 4, it was announced that the Police Statue would be restored.

After the Statue was bombed again on Oct. 6, 1970, the plaque was pulled off, presumably by persons on the conservative right. The holes for the bolts that once held this plaque are still visible.

10. FORMER SITE OF DESPLAINES STREET POLICE STATION (West side of Desplaines, midway between Randolph and Washington)

Until the 1950's, the Desplaines Street Police Station was a major landmark in this area. A parking lot now occupies the site.

It was in the alley next to the station, that the 176 policemen awaited orders from Ward and Bonfield to march into the square, and here Mayor Carter Harrison told Bonfield to send all the police home, since there was no evidence of trouble from the meeting.

Bonfield had been spying on Mayor Harrison throughout the meeting. The Mayor returned briefly to the meeting, and then went home. Bonfield had received the report that the Mayor had finally left, and then he marched on the meeting. Mayor Harrison heard the bomb blast from his home on Ashland Avenue, and rushed back to the station again.

The Desplaines Street Police Station and the alley where the 176 policemen gathered.

It was the custom sometimes to use police stations for housing the homeless. During the many depressions of the 1870's and 1880's, many starving workers were kept here according to Albert Parsons who wrote the following in March of 1885:

"In this city of Chicago there are 35,000 men, women and children in a starving condition, driven by enforced idleness to live upon charity or seek the suicide's grave. In the Desplaines Street Station alone, through the terribly cold winter nights, as many as 400 homeless, destitute men sought shelter and slept upon the cold, bare flagstones of the prison cell, receiving in the morning at 5 o'clock a bowl of hot soup, containing a slice of bread, for their breakfast, and then turned out upon the street to continue their vain search for employment. Others, who after midnight were turned out of the warm saloons where they had sought shelter, were driven to the cold damp tunnels, where they trotted up and down all night to keep from freezing to death."

After the bombing, from the descriptions of those who were there at the time, the station was like a field hospital, with Dr. Henrotin and others looking after the many who were brought here.

NOTE: Return to your car at this point, driving by sites 11 through 20.

11. INTERSECTION OF HALSTED AND RANDOLPH

Today this section of Haymarket Square is still active. Wholesale markets line both sides of Randolph to Ashland, selling flowers, vegetables, fish, evergreens, and everything imaginable. Farmers can no longer sell direct to the individual. One farmer in 1975 tried to do it and was ticketed and fined by the city. Today, the railroads, middlemen, and grocery chains frown on direct selling. However, many cooperative groups and buyers clubs come here to buy in quantity in order to get food at lower prices.

12. FORMER SITE OF STREETCAR STOP (Southwest corner of Randolph and Halsted)

On the night of Haymarket the Parsons family and their guest Lizzie Holmes walked from their home on Grand Avenue to Halsted and to this corner on their way to the Alarm office on Wells Street.

Parsons knew nothing about the Haymarket meeting, but was on his way to his wife's meeting of the sewing workers. A reporter, Mr. Owen, ran into Parsons and described the scene as follows:

"I saw Parsons at the corner of Randolph and Halsted streets shortly before 8 o'clock; I asked him where the meeting was going to be held; he said he did not know anything about the meeting. I asked him whether he was going to speak. He said: No, he was going over to the South Side. Mrs. Parsons and some children came up just then, and Mr. Parsons before entering the street car, slapped me familiarly upon the back and asked me if I was armed, and I said no. I asked him: 'Have you any dynamite about you?' He laughed, and Mrs. Parsons said: 'He is a very dangerous-looking man, isn't he?' And they got on the car and went east. . . ."

Several other people must have seen Parsons and told August Spies about it. This is why Spies sent a messenger here to find Parsons before opening the meeting himself.

13. BARNEY'S MARKET CLUB RESTAURANT (Southeast corner of Halsted and Randolph)

As you turn south at the corner of Randolph and Halsted you will find the colorful and historic eating place of the Haymarket, Barney's.

Many notable people came here, and were insulted if they were not addressed by a title; therefore, today, everyone who comes into Barney's is addressed as "Senator".

14. WASHINGTON STREET TUNNEL (Washington and Clinton)

Turning east at Washington Street and traveling three blocks toward the Loop, we approach the historic old Washington Street Tunnel which was built in 1869 at a cost of over $500,000. It was built as a pedestrian walkway and later was used for streetcars, since the raising of the river bridges frequently interfered with traffic. The tunnel was originally 1,608 feet long and was considered an engineering marvel at the time. During the depression of 1873 the poor slept in this tunnel to escape the cold.

Today the tunnel is blocked off, but the Parsons family, Lizzie Holmes, and Samuel Fielden hurried through this tunnel to reach the Haymarket meeting in order to help August Spies.

15. FORMER SITE OF MARKET SQUARE (Now Wacker between Madison and Washington)

After crossing the river on Washington Blvd., we come to Wacker Drive. On your right along what is now Wacker Drive was the old Market Square, another of Chicago's open market areas of the past. You will only catch a glimpse of this area in front of the Civic Opera House, but this is an important site in Chicago labor history.

It was in this square next to the river, once surrounded by the offices of foreign language newspapers, union offices, and shipping docks, that Albert Parsons spoke during the Railroad Strike of 1877. It was Parsons' speech on July 23 here that resulted in his being fired by the Chicago Times and blacklisted throughout Chicago.

By July 28, 1877, the police were allowing no public meetings in Chicago and Parsons witnessed the following scene in the Market Square:

"That night a peaceable meeting of 3,000 workingmen was dispersed on Market street, near Madison. I witnessed it. Over 100 policemen charged upon this peaceable mass-meeting, firing their pistols and clubbing right and left. The printers, the iron-molders, and other trade unions which had held regular monthly or weekly meetings of their unions for years past, when they came to their hall-doors now for that purpose, found policemen standing there, the doors barred, and the members told that all meetings had been prohibited by the Chief of Police."

On Thanksgiving Day, 1885 a "Poor Peoples March" began in the Market Square:

"At the hour named several hundred men and women assembled at the corner of Washington and Market streets, where a large red flag wavered from the top of a pile of salt-barrels which covered the sidewalk. By the time the meeting was called to order, some 2,000 persons stood in the mud and slush, and cold, piercing wind which was the ideal of a raw, chilly November day . . . A. R. Parsons mounted a pile of salt-barrels, and using them as a stand, was introduced as the first speaker."

The Market Square was almost the site of the meeting on May 4, 1886 instead of the Haymarket (See No. 1 for a discussion of this).

16. SITE OF CITY HALL AND FORMER SITE OF CENTRAL POLICE HEADQUARTERS (Entire block bound by Washington, Randolph, Clark, and LaSalle)

On your left as you drive along Washington Street is the present City Hall and County Building. There have been many City Halls on this site. The present building dates from 1901. The building in 1886 did not cover the entire block but was shaped like a barbell with the narrow part in the middle containing the Central Police Headquarters.

It was here that Frederick Ebersold, General Superintendent of Police, had his headquarters along with his Secretary and Chief Inspector, Bonfield. It was in the jail under this building that August Spies, Fielden, Lingg, and Neebe and several others were first kept until their transfer to the County Jail (See No. 21).

Inspector Bonfield and Chief Ebersold did not get along well together and neither of them got along with Captain Schaack of the Chicago Avenue Station (See No. 32). Both Bonfield and Schaack wanted Ebersold's job and were out for publicity and support from the business community.

In an interview in the Daily News three years after Haymarket on May 10, 1889, Ebersold made the following admission about Captain Schaack:

"It was my policy to quiet matters down as soon as possible after the 4th of May. The general unsettled state of things was an in-

jury to Chicago . . . On the other hand, Capt. Schaack wanted to keep things stirring. He wanted bombs to be found here, there, all around, everywhere, I thought people would lie down and sleep better if they were not afraid that their home would be blown to pieces any minute. But this man Schaack, the little boy who must have glory or his heart would be broken, wanted none of this policy. Now, here is something the public does not know. After we got the Anarchist societies broken up, Schaack wanted to send out men to again organize new societies right away. You see what this would do. He wanted to keep the thing boiling . . . keep himself prominent before the public. Well, I sat down on that: I didn't believe in such work and of course Schaack didn't like it. . . . After I heard all that, I began to think there was, perhaps, not so much to all this Anarchist business as they claimed . . ."

The City Hall (Washington Street looking east) and the entrance to the Central Police Headquarters (lower left-hand corner). Altgeld's Unity Building can be seen above the building in the center of this picture. (Courtesy Chicago Historical Society)

17. UNITY BUILDING (Now 131 N. Dearborn Street)

Turning left on to Dearborn Street just past the Picasso Statue and opposite the Civic Center, one passes the old Unity Building, one of Chicago's earliest skyscrapers, which was built by Governor John Peter Altgeld.

Altgeld named it the Unity Building because he felt that was what Chicago needed . . . "unity" of the many ethnic groups of the city that were being played against each other for cheap labor by the business community.

After Altgeld pardoned Neebe, Fielden, and Schwab from Joliet Penitentiary all the businessmen and lawyers moved out of this building, and only charity organizations stayed in the building. Charles Yerkes, the Chicago "Streetcar King", reportedly offered Altgeld a half million dollar bribe not to veto a transit bill Yerkes wanted passed; but Altgeld refused and vetoed the bill. Then Yerkes and businessmen who were angry with Altgeld for the Haymarket pardon and the Governor's protest against President Cleveland's action against the Pullman workers, got the banks to call in Altgeld's mortgages on the Unity Building. Altgeld went bankrupt and lost his beloved Unity Building. Altgeld's former protege, Clarence Darrow, offered Altgeld a partnership in his law firm, and this income would be all that Altgeld had until his death in 1902.

During the construction of the Unity an engineer made a mistake, and the entire building leans at a slight angle.

This building was also Democratic Party Headquarters in 1892 when Altgeld won the governorship in Illinois' first secret ballot election. Altgeld had walked throughout southern Illinois in this election in order to get support from the downstate farmers, who feared the large railroad interests which were bankrupting them.

18. FORMER SITE OF SOUTH WATER STREET MARKET (Now Wacker Drive between Lake and Michigan Avenue)

Proceed up Dearborn Street. It was to the corner of Lake and Dearborn that Parsons walked on the evening of July 24, 1877 past troops who were camped here to be used against the workers at the time of the Railroad Strike.

We soon arrive at Wacker Drive which runs along the south bank of the Chicago River.

Wacker Drive was once known as the South Water Street Market, but this area was cleared on August 27, 1925 as a part of the Burnham Plan for Chicago. All the truck farmers were forced out. The entire area was leveled, since many businessmen feared this area as a breeding ground for crime, especially since it was located only a few blocks from City Hall and Marshall Field's store. Market areas such as this were also used for rallies of workers and the businessmen feared another Haymarket.

Even the name South Water Street has disappeared except for a short block from Wabash to Michigan. Although the farmers were promised that they could continue selling their produce on the lower level of Wacker Drive, and it was designed for that purpose, all the small growers were gradually pushed out.

Today the market area around 15th Street between Morgan and Racine avenues, which was built in the late 1920's retains the name South Water Street Market, but it is a long way from City Hall now.

19. MARINA CITY TWIN TOWERS (300 North State Street... Between Dearborn and State on the Chicago River)

These buildings were built in 1964 by the Building Service Employees Union with their pension funds in response to Mayor Daley's desire to bring families back to the central core of the city.

The architect Bertrand Goldberg designed these two 80 story buildings to include 18 stories of parking, restaurants, a bank, theatres, ice-skating, and a boat marina. Although originally intended to have efficiency apartments starting at less than $100, the building design and location created such a demand that rents went sky high and the idea of middle income workers living here was never realized. Eventually the Service Employees Union sold the building.

Marina City along with the Fewkes Tower (See No. 33) and Harper Square in Hyde Park, which was built by the Amalgamated Clothing Workers (See No. 93), are examples of how unions today are still involved in helping their members, are concerned with urban problems, and working for social change. These are the very things that Parsons and the other Haymarket Martyrs were advocating in 1886.

Architecturally the buildings are of slab construction with circular discs resting on a central core column. It is also an example of Frank Lloyd Wright's core-cantilever construction.

Four workmen lost their lives and six were seriously injured during the construction of this innovative building.

20. MARINA CITY OFFICE BUILDING, WCFL RADIO, AND THE OFFICES OF THE CHICAGO FEDERATION OF LABOR (300 N. State . . . Between Dearborn and State)

The Marina City Office Building, just north of the twin towers, houses on its top floor the offices of the Chicago Federation of Labor, which grew out of the Trades and Labor Assembly that was originally founded by Albert Parsons.

Unlike the situation in 1886, labor in Chicago today has a great deal of influence politically and economically; but it has taken the Chicago labor movement over 100 years of struggle to achieve this goal.

In March of 1923 the Executive Board of the Chicago Federation of Labor began discussion on the establishment of a radio station.

Both President John Fitzpatrick and Secretary Edward Nockels of the Federation believed a radio station was necessary to tell labor's story. They believed it was necessary to fight the anti-labor papers that were creating the "Red Scare" of the 1920's, the same papers that had spread the hysteria that lead to the execution of the Haymarket Martyrs.

However, it was difficult to do this since NBC and CBS were trying to prevent the establishment of small stations so they would have a monopoly. The Chicago Federation of Labor took this case to the courts and they won, paving the way for the establishment of many small stations. On July 27, 1926 WCFL, "The Voice of Labor", went on the air for the first time. This station was of great importance throughout the Depression years of the 1930's in helping to organize workers and tell their story.

Profits from WCFL are used to keep down the per capita tax on union members used to support the Chicago Federation of Labor. Television service may be added to the station's services.

WCFL and WEVD, named after Eugene Victor Debs and located in the New York Metropolitan area, are unique since they are the only two labor stations in America.

NOTE: Drive up Dearborn to Hubbard street and park. (Parking may be difficult on weekdays)

21. FORMER COOK COUNTY COURT HOUSE
(Northwest Corner of Dearborn and Hubbard)

You have now reached the sites connected with the historic Haymarket Trial and Execution.

Although the original Cook County Court House was torn down in 1892 and rebuilt as a larger structure, some of the original stone was reused. From the picture on page 47 you can see how the original building once looked.

Today this structure is known as the Hubbard Street Police Station. In 1929 a much larger Court House was built on California Avenue, and this building served for a time as the offices of the Board of Health. This building was the setting of the play "Front Page" by Ben Hecht and Charles MacArthur, originally written in 1928 and made into a film in 1931 and 1974.

The trial that was held inside the Court House was a farce and one of the most unjust trials in American history. The jury was hand picked by a special bailiff, Henry L. Ryce, instead of being drawn by lot as was customary. As a result of this trial the system of juror selection would be changed, but this reform was too late to save the lives of the Haymarket Martyrs.

The trial opened on June 21, 1886 with only seven of the Haymarket Eight in custody. As the trial opened, however, Albert Parsons dramatically turned himself in to be tried with his comrades.

The Cook County Court House as it looked at the time of the Haymarket Trial (Courtesy Chicago Historical Society)

It took 21 days to select the 12 jurors and over 981 people were examined. One prospective juror who expressed some sympathy for the defendants in the courtroom was later fired by his employer.

The Haymarket Eight could find no lawyer who wished to defend them, and finally their friend Dr. Schmidt asked an attorney named Captain William Black to look for someone. Since Black could not find another attorney to take the case he finally consented to take it himself, although he realized his career would be ruined . . . and it was. Later, Black got three other attorneys to assist him . . . Sigismond Zeisler, Moses Salomon, and William Foster.

Although Black had hoped that Judge Murray F. Tuley would be assigned to the case, instead Judge Joseph E. Gary was put in charge. Throughout the trial, Judge Gary invited pretty young debutantes to join him on the bench. One young lady later stated that Judge Gary had joked with her and spent most of his time drawing pictures instead of paying attention to the testimony. Even when the State's Attorney told the judge that they wished to drop the charges against Oscar Neebe, Judge Gary gave him 15 years in Joliet Prison at hard labor.

It became obvious throughout the trial that these men were not being tried for what they did, but for what they were saying. State's Attorney Grinnel stated this bluntly in his summation on August 11:

"Law is upon trial. Anarchy is on trial. These men have been selected, picked out by the grand jury. They are no more guilty than the thousands who follow them . . . Convict these men, make examples of them, hang them, and you save our institutions."

The trial finally ended on August 20, and it was obvious that the City of Chicago wanted revenge for the death of *seven* policemen. When *seven* of the Haymarket Eight were given the death penalty it seemed more like the Old Testament "an eye for an eye . . ." than justice.

After sentencing, each of the defendants was allowed to comment on his sentence. Albert Parsons delivered a brilliant rebuttal that lasted eight hours and it was given over a two day period. It was later printed and circulated throughout the country.

In April of 1893, Judge Gary defended his conduct in the trial in an article in Century Magazine:

"Mixed with all the approval of my own part in conviction of the anarchists that has come to my eyes and ears, the amount of which is beyond my summing up, there has been an undertone, like a strain in music, that the anarchists deserved their fate; that society has the right to enforce the first law of nature . . . self-preservation; and therefore if I had a little strained the law, or administered it with great rigor against them, I was to be commended for my doing so."

Eventually Gary was removed from the bench for his unfair handling of several later cases.

22. VIEW EAST ON HUBBARD STREET

The area along Hubbard Street still has the look and feel of the 1880's. Hubbard Street was once called Michigan Street, but when Michigan Avenue was extended across the river in the 1920's the name was changed because of the confusion.

East of Dearborn the old buildings have been preserved by Harry Weese and Associates, (10 W. Hubbard) who planted the trees along the street east of the station. This architectural firm, that built many of Chicago's new skyscrapers, has tried to preserve this area.

Try to imagine the crowds that thronged the streets each morning as the jury entered the Court House, and the reporters from all over the world here to cover the case.

23. FORMER SITE OF COOK COUNTY JAIL (Now a Chicago Firehouse of Engine Co. 42. . . . Southwest corner of Dearborn and Illinois)

For many years this was the site of the notorious Cook County Jail. It was finally replaced by new facilities on California Ave. in 1929, now also old and overcrowded. The buildings on this site were finally torn down in 1936, and for many years it was a vacant lot. In the early 1970's a beautiful new firehouse was built on the site.

Not only did this jail hold the Haymarket Eight throughout the trial, but later Eugene Debs was confined here after the Pullman Strike. "Big Bill" Haywood also spent six months here after the Palmer Raids in 1917-1918.

After the trial was over, Neebe was removed to Joliet Prison, but the other seven remained here awaiting an appeal of their case to the Illinois Supreme Court and the U.S. Supreme Court.

Generally, the men's spirits were high, except for Engel who only spoke German and scarcely knew what was happening throughout the trial. Engel's young daughter visited him often to try to cheer him up.

August Spies had visits from the beautiful Nina Van Zandt, whom he would later marry (See No. 31).

Fischer's wife and three children were allowed to see him up until the last day before the execution.

The young and very athletic Louis Lingg enjoyed showing off for visitors by swinging from the bars of his cell.

Albert Parsons was visited by his many friends and his wife Lucy, when she wasn't off speaking and raising money for his defense.

Eventually Spies, Fielden, and Schwab asked for clemency from the governor, but Parsons refused to ask under any circumstances. Later Spies renounced his earlier petition and therefore his sentence was not commuted to life. After being given a life sentence, on November 10, 1887, Fielden and Schwab were sent to Joliet Prison with Neebe.

When Parsons was asked by his attorney William Black to sign a pardon petition to the Governor of Illinois, Parsons said the following:

"Captain, I know that you are right. I know that if I should sign this application for pardon my sentence would be commuted. No longer ago than Sunday night Melville E. Stone, the editor of the Daily News, spent nearly two hours in my cell, urging me to sign a petition, and assuring me that if I would do so I should have his influence and the influence of his paper in favor of commutation of my sentence; and I know that that means my sentence would be commuted. But I will not do it . . . I am an innocent man. . . innocent of this offense of which I have been found guilty by the jury. . . I can afford to be hung for the sake of the ideas I hold and the cause I have espoused if the people of the State of Illinois can afford to hang an innocent man who voluntarily placed himself in their power"

Parsons told Black that if he signed a petition and deserted Engel, Lingg, and Fischer they would not have a chance.

Since Parsons had turned himself in and was a native-born American of distinguished family background, many wished him to be pardoned. But Engel, Lingg, and Fischer were German born and German speaking, and the public had no sympathy for them.

When Parsons wrote to his wife, Lucy, he always referred to the jail as the "Cook County Bastile-Cell #29". Parsons and the others were kept in the second floor of cells until November 9 when they were moved downstairs. Parsons was moved to cell 7, but for some strange reason Lingg was separated from the rest.

On the morning of November 10, 1887, at 8:45 a.m. on the very day that he might have been pardoned by the Governor (Samuel Gompers was in Springfield appealing the case for the five that were to die the next day), Louis Lingg was mysteriously found dead in his cell. His face had been blown away by a dynamite cap.

The police said that his girl friend, Ida Miller, had smuggled the cap to him, but she had not visited him for several days. Lingg's cell had been searched several times since her visit and he had been stripped and searched as well, so it seems impossible that the cap hadn't been found.

The Neebe family always believed that the police gave him a cigar that morning with a dynamite cap in it, since by Nov. 10, 1887 the public attitude was beginning to change toward the execution. His supposed suicide was used to propagandize the guilt of the other four.

Lingg, who was only 21 years old and very strong physically, lived until afternoon despite the fact that most of his face was gone. His death made headlines around the world, and a Barnum-type road show offered thousands of dollars for his body which they wanted to preserve and place on show for tourists. The Engel family, to whom the body was given, refused.

24. SITE OF EXECUTION (Alley between Hubbard Street Station and the Firehouse)

This alley was once a courtyard between the Cook County Court House and the County Jail with a large door at the alley entrance at Dearborn Street. (See the picture on page 52). The gallows were erected in this courtyard, and the men could hear the hammers and sawing from their cells.

The night before the execution all slept well, and Albert Parsons sang his favorite song "Anne Laurie" in his cell. Later they would all sing the French Marseillaise as they marched to their death.

All rose early and were allowed to have anything they wished for breakfast. When Parsons was asked if he wished stimulants he answered:

"No. I wish to go off sober, and perhaps the temperance people will be disposed to drop a single tear of sympathy in consequence."

When asked what he did want Parsons said:

"I would prefer a cup of coffee".

Then a pot of coffee and a bowl of crackers was brought. He drank the coffee and ate a few of the crackers, and thanked the deputy and then said:

"Now I feel all right. Let's finish the business."

At about 11:30 a.m. on Nov. 11, 1887, a day that would be known later as "Black Friday" around the world, Sheriff Matson, Jailer Folz, the Cook County physician, and several deputies appeared first at August Spies' cell and then went to each of the other three cells. The death sentence was read and the men were marched to the courtyard and on to the scaffold surrounded with two hundred people who had been invited to watch.

A reporter described the scene in this way:

"With complete unconcern, the four took their positions on the trap. The nooses were placed around their necks. Fischer helped to adjust his. Spies' was too tight. He smiled a 'Thank You' when it was made more comfortable. Spies then cried out . . . "There will come a time when our silence will be more powerful than the voices you strangle today'. Fischer and Engel said . . . 'Hurrah for anarchy' and Engel added . . . 'This is the happiest moment of my life.' Parsons was the last to speak . . . he said, 'Will I be allowed to speak, O men of America? Let me speak, Sheriff Matson! Let the voice of the people be heard!

Then the trap was sprung a few minutes before noon."

The execution of the Haymarket Martyrs (left to right) Spies, Fischer, Engel, Parsons

Runners took the news up Dearborn street to the many newspaper offices that once lined this street south of Madison. Marshall Field, Pullman, Armour, Crane, and many other businessmen who had fought even the commutations of Fielden and Schwab must have sighed a breath of relief that these four were finally dead after a delay of over one year.

25. HUBBARD STREET WEST OF DEARBORN

Although this street is quiet today, one can imagine the scene on the morning of November 11, 1887 when the street was roped off for a block around the jail. Bulletins were posted on each corner to let the crowd know what was happening.

The County Jail and the alley gate on the day of the execution

Outside on the streets there were many angry people. The police feared a possible revolution of the ethnic groups within Chicago. Friends of the Haymarket Martyrs had offered to try to capture the jail and free them, but the four men had pledged them not to do this. Everyone was tense! One businessman said that "trade downtown was duller today than it has ever been".

Lucy Parsons had hoped to see Albert the night before for the last time, but she was told to come back early the next day. The next morning she arrived with the children and her good friend Lizzie Holmes. Mrs. Holmes described dramatically what happened:

"Every street for two blocks away leading towards the jail was crossed by a rope and guarded by a line of police armed with Winchester rifles. At the first corner Mrs. Parsons quietly made known her errand. The lieutenant said she could not go in there, but that she should pass on to the next corner, and the officer there would perhaps let her through. She did so with the same result . . . They then sent her from corner to corner, never telling her she could not go in. Always telling her to see someone else. Meanwhile the precious moments were flying; sweet little Lulu's face was blue with cold, and her beautiful eyes were swimming with tears. Manly little Albert, too, was shivering in the raw atmosphere, as he patiently followed his grief-stricken mother from one warlike street to another.

Lucy asked an officer to just take the children in to see their father for the last time, but she was told to move along. Finally Lucy tried to go through the line saying 'to kill her as they were murdering her husband.' "

Lucy, the children, and Lizzie Holmes were then arrested by the police and hustled into a patrol wagon and taken to the Chicago Avenue Police Station which was under the control of Captain Schaack (See No. 32 for what happened at the station).

26. FORMER SITE OF REVERE HOUSE HOTEL
(Southeast Corner of Hubbard and Clark)

In a hotel, directly across from the Criminal Court the jurors were sequestered throughout the trial. They lived here for two months and each morning crossed the street to the court room escorted by the police.

The Revere House was so expensive in 1886 that many newspapers criticized the courts for the tremendous cost of the meals and rooms that were being paid for by the public. By the 1920's the Revere House had become a theatrical hangout of questionable reputation. Later known as the Capitol, it was demolished in April, 1976.

A great deal has been written since 1886 about the attitudes of the jury toward the Haymarket Eight at the time of their selection. Theodore Denker, a shipping clerk for Henry W. King & Co., stated that he believed the Haymarket Eight guilty.

John B. Greiner, a clerk of the Northwestern Railroad, said that *"it is evident that the defendants are connected with that affair from their being there."*

G.W. Adams, a traveling salesman and painting contractor, admitted he formed an opinion from the newspapers already and that he had discussed the case with his friends.

H.T. Sanford, a clerk of the Northwestern Railroad in the Freight Auditor's Office (See No. 95 for more about Sanford), when asked if he had a prejudice against Socialists and Communists, said, *"Yes, sir; a decided prejudice."*

Twenty-four hours before the jury retired to consider the verdict, the Chicago Tribune opened its columns for solicitation of voluntary contributions to reward the jury. It was suggested by the Tribune that a sum of $100,000 should be raised for this purpose. Immediately letters and money began to arrive.

E.A. Mulford contributed money to the Tribune fund and wrote:

"The long agony is over. Law has triumphed. . . The 'Twelve good men and true', whose honesty and fearlessness made a conviction possible should not be forgotten. Let them be generously remembered. Raise a fund. . . to be presented with the thanks of a grateful people."

27. STEINMUELLER'S HALL (Now 406-408 Clark Street, American China and Glassware Company)

Across from the Capitol Hotel is a building which was once known as Steinmueller's Hall. This building and hall is typical of dozens of such halls that once lined Clark Street. They usually had saloons on the first floor and large meeting halls on the second.

It was in this building in May of 1878 that the Socialistic Labor Party of which Albert Parsons was a member, had a meeting in order to consummate the purchase of the Arbeiter-Zeitung newspaper.

It was decided to issue notes at 6% interest, payable as soon as the Socialist Party had secured enough from collections and other sources. Oscar Neebe bought two dollars worth of shares. It was because he owned these shares that had purchased the printing presses that announced the Haymarket Meeting at which the policemen were killed, that Neebe received 15 years in Joliet Prison.

28. FORMER SITE OF ULRICH'S HALL (Southwest corner of Clark and Kinzie—Now Thompson Cafeteria Building)

Ulrich's Hall was another of the Clark Street meeting halls. Many unions met here monthly and this hall was the scene in

1894 of the National Convention of the American Railway Union. It was here that Rev. Carwardine and Jennie Curtis spoke to the delegates, and asked Eugene Debs and the convention to support the striking workers of Pullman.

Eugene Debs lived across the street at the Revere House for part of the time during the convention, and it was there he was served the injunction demanding he send all the Pullman strikers back to work.

After another unjust trial in 1895, Debs was sent to a jail in Woodstock, Illinois out of fear that the workers of Chicago might try to free him if he was sent to the County Jail.

29. LA SALLE STREET TUNNEL, SCENE OF THE "BREAD RIOT" (Middle of LaSalle Street at Kinzie)

This is all that remains of the historic LaSalle Street Tunnel that was opened on July 1, 1871. It was originally 1,854 feet long and was built at a cost of $566,276.48. For years this tunnel made it possible for people to get from the south to the north side of the river when all the bridges were turned or raised, and this tunnel was a major escape route during the Chicago Fire. When Wacker Drive was built in the 1920's, the south entrance was closed off. The north end is still used for parking and an entrance to the City Parking Lot on LaSalle Street.

This tunnel was the scene of the "Bread Riot" during the Winter of 1872-73 when thousands were starving as a result of the Great Fire and the depression that followed.

Instead of receiving help from the offices of the Relief and Aid Society at LaSalle and Randolph, the protesting workers were driven into this tunnel by Deputy Joseph Dixon. The police closed in from both sides and clubbed, beat, and killed several trapped in the tunnel. Leading businessmen had been borrowing money from the relief funds at little or no interest for the redevelopment of their businesses. Parsons arrived in Chicago about this time and later wrote:

"In 1874 I became interested in the 'labor question', growing out of the effort made by Chicago working people at that time to compel the 'Relief and Aid Society' to render to the suffering poor of the city an account of the vast sums of money (several millions of dollars) held by that society and contributed by the whole world to relieve the distress occasioned by the great Chicago Fire of 1871.

"It was claimed by the working people that the money was being used for purposes foreign to the intention of the donors; that rings of speculators were corruptly using the money, while the distressed and impoverished people for whom it was contributed were denied its use. . . . I began to examine into this subject, and I found that the complaints of the working people against the society were just and proper."

NOTE: Return to your car at this point, driving by sites 30 through 57.

30. FORMER SITE OF BRANDT'S HALL (Formerly at southeast corner of Erie and Clark)

Although this site is not visible from Dearborn, when you have reached Erie you are only one block east of the former site of historic Brandt's Hall. The hall was demolished in the early 1970's for a parking area behind a Union 76 Service Station.

Brandt's Hall was the scene on June 27, 1905 of the founding convention of the Industrial Workers of the World, better known as the Wobblies or I.W.W. Among the two hundred delegates meeting at Brandt's Hall were Lucy Parsons, Mother Jones, Eugene Debs, Daniel DeLeon, William Trautmann, and William "Big Bill" Haywood.

Mother Jones spoke to the delegates asking them to form "One Big Union". Haywood called this meeting the "Continental Congress" of the working class of America (See No. 113 for more about Haywood).

On the last day of the convention, Lucy Parsons asked all the delegates to go out to the Martyrs' Monument in German Waldheim Cemetery, and to dedicate themselves to the principles for which the Haymarket Martyrs had died.

31. FORMER SITE OF THE HOME OF NINA VAN ZANDT (Demolished, formerly near the Southwest corner of Huron and Rush)

Although this site is not visible from Dearborn when you reach Huron Street you are three blocks west of the former home of Nina Van Zandt. The site is now a plaza for the Headquarters of the Episcopal Church.

Miss Nina Van Zandt, the daughter of a wealthy Chicago chemist, visited the trial during the summer of 1886 like many other society women. She came both in the morning and the afternoon, always wearing a different dress. The Chicago papers even began carrying stories about what she wore each day.

Nina fell in love with Spies from a distance during the trial, and then went to see him in his cell. Spies came to enjoy her visits and finally agreed to marriage. They were married by proxy during the trial, with Spies' brother standing up for him, since his jailors refused to allow the marriage in his cell.

The Van Zandt family lived around the corner from the McCormick family and in 1952 Colonel McCormick of the Tribune recalled Haymarket:

"I was born on July 30, 1880. My first vivid recollection is the day that the anarchists were hanged in Chicago, November 11, 1887. Children were not allowed out of doors because riots were feared. The police were armed with rifles.

The widow of one of the men, Miss Van Zandt, who married the anarchist Spies by proxy after his conviction, lived in our neighborhood. We were deadly afraid of the poor woman and I am afraid I shouted at her on the street."

The morning of the execution Nina and her mother rode down Huron and south on Dearborn toward the jail to see August Spies for the last time. They were stopped by the police. They turned the carriage around, returned to the house, and closed all the window drapes. People heard screams and cries from the house. There were false reports in Chicago papers that Nina had killed herself. (For more information on Nina see No. 114)

32. LAWSON YMCA (Northeast corner of Dearborn and Chicago Avenue)
EAST CHICAGO AVENUE POLICE STATION (113 Chicago Avenue, 1 ½ blocks west of Dearborn)

Going north on Dearborn you see at Chicago Avenue the skyscraper YMCA named after Victor Fremont Lawson, owner of the Chicago Daily News at the time of the Haymarket Affair. This building was built in 1931 after Lawson's death in 1925 when he gave several million dollars to the YMCA for the improvement of their buildings and facilities.

Lawson made his fortune by practicing "yellow journalism." It was the sensational Daily News story of the police attack near the McCormick Reaper Plant that led Spies to believe that six workers had been killed instead of two.

The Daily News, like the Times and Tribune often called for dynamite to be used against the workers. Articles from these papers were not allowed to be read to the jury, but similar articles from the Arbeiter-Zeitung and Alarm were used to justify the execution of the Haymarket Martyrs.

The "hymn singing" Lawson was a friend of Dwight Moody (See No. 41) and like Moody thought that workers should be interested in salvation instead of an eight hour day and better working conditions.

Lawson was a member of the YMCA Board in Chicago. J.V. Farwell, President of the YMCA of North America was typically unrestrained in his comment on the Haymarket case:

"I am proud of our Government. Its beauty and power over all other Governments is demonstrated by the conviction of these Anarchist fiends. . . Why, even Russia is left behind, for while she sends them to Siberian mines. . . It was left for our glorious America to teach them all a lesson in how to exterminate this social vermin by chopping off its head, and thus kill the body of the movement."

Although not visible from Dearborn Street the Chicago Avenue Police Station is still located a block and a half west of Dearborn. The original building has been replaced by a new modern structure. This area was the Police District of Captain Schaack. It was Schaack who rounded up hundreds of labor leaders after Haymarket. He broke into homes without search warrants and dragged people out of their beds. He later wrote a sensational book titled, "Anarchy and Anarchists," which was circulated by the Pinkerton Detective Agency to encourage companies to hire spies.

In 1889, it was discovered by the Chicago Times, by then owned by the liberal former mayor Carter Harrison, that both Inspector Bonfield and Captain Schaack were receiving payoffs from local tavern owners and prostitutes in this area.

When the Times exposed this story on Jan. 5, 1889, Schaack had the editor of the Times arrested and thrown in jail and the presses closed down. This was exactly what he had done to the labor press in 1886. But this was too much, and businessmen in Chicago finally demanded that both Bonfield and Schaack be removed from the police department. Eventually they were.

It was discovered that Lingg's gold cuff links, which he had wished to be given to his sweetheart, Ida Miller, had been taken by Schaack. A great deal of stolen merchandise was found in the homes of the policemen from Schaack's district. It also was uncovered that Schaack and his men were receiving payments from a fund of $475,000 that had been set up by Chicago businessmen, including Marshall Field and George Pullman, to uncover communists and subversives.

The Chicago Avenue Police Station in 1886.

It was to this station that Lucy Parsons, her children, and Lizzie Holmes were brought on the morning of the execution. Lizzie Holmes dramatically described what happened to them when they arrived there:

"Far from being given arm chairs in a comfortable office, we were locked up in dark, dirty stone cells—Mrs. Parsons and her children in one, myself in another.

And there—shame be it to America that I have it to relate! There we were stripped to the skin and searched! Even the children, crying with fright, were undressed and carefully searched . . . .

The woman ran her fingers through my hair, through the hems of my skirts, the gathers of my undergarments, even to my stockings; I asked her what she expected to find. 'I don't know' she simpered, 'this is my duty'. She clanged the doors behind her finally and we were left alone . . . .

At a few minutes past twelve the matron came and said coldly: 'It is all over', and left us.

Not a soul came and asked the bereaved woman if they could help her to even a cup of cold water. And I, the one friend near her, could only sit shivering with my face pressed to the cruel iron bars, listening to her low, despairing moans . . . .

. . . At three o'clock Capt. Schaack came down and asked how long we had been there, hypocritically expressed sorrow that we

had been locked up, and opened our prison doors. They had done their worst and Mrs. Parsons was permitted to go to her desolated home."

33. FEWKES TOWER (Southwest corner of Dearborn and Chestnut)

Going north on Dearborn you pass on your left a prize winning 30 story building built by the Chicago Teachers Union in 1967. It is named after John Fewkes, a former President of Local 1 of the American Federation of Teachers. Originally built for retired teachers, it is now rented to people in many different fields.

Jane Addams and John Dewey formed the Teachers' Federation in 1896 toward the close of the administration of Governor Altgeld. The same businessmen who were demanding the execution of the Haymarket Eight were not paying their fair share of taxes to the schools. Pullman property worth over $10 million was assessed at only $15,000. The Teachers' Federation carried this tax case to the Illinois Supreme Court and won.

After losing the case many businessmen on the Chicago School Board wanted the new tax income to go toward school construction and kick-backs to contractors who were their friends. The Teachers' Federation fought for more and better trained teachers, smaller classes, and better textbooks. The Teachers' Federation eventually became the Chicago Federation of Teachers Local 1, the very first local of the American Federation of Teachers, still fighting for teachers' rights to democracy on the job and a decent education for young people.

34. HEADQUARTERS OF THE SALVATION ARMY (Southwest corner of Dearborn and Delaware)

A short distance north of Fewkes Tower is the Central Region Headquarters of the Salvation Army.

For several years after Haymarket, parades, marches, demonstrations of any kind, and street-corner speeches were outlawed. This law particularly hit the Salvation Army, and many Army members were arrested for their religious street rallies.

Finally the Salvation Army, labor unions, and various liberal organizations worked together to get these laws repealed, and Chicagoans again had the right to practice freedom of speech and assembly.

35. FORMER HOME OF THE DILL PICKLE CLUB (863 Dearborn, Northeast corner of Dearborn and Tooker Place)

Across the street from the Salvation Army Headquarters in an old brownstone mansion some of the greatest writers, poets, playwrites, and liberal thinkers in America once gathered.

The Dill Pickle Club began meeting here in 1919. Among its members were Ben Hecht, Charles MacArthur, Carl Sandburg, Theodore Dreiser, Dr. Preston Bradley, and Sherwood Anderson. Dr. Ben Reitman (See No. 105) was known as the "Reverend" of the club.

The main entrance was through the alley which is known as W. Tooker Place. The alley was originally closed off at the end like an English Mews, and many artists and writers had their studios here.

Notice a door about two-thirds of the way up the alley. This was the entrance to the club. The door was originally painted orange with a green light over it and these words were painted on the door:

"Step High, Stoop Low, Leave Your Dignity Outside"

If you look above the door you'll see a window with shutters. This was once the apartment of Ernest Hemingway. While living in this neighborhood, Hemingway wrote "The Killers," later made into a movie in the 1940's. "The Killers" was about "Swede", a Scandinavian worker and fighter who lived along Chicago Avenue, a street that was known for years as "Swede Broadway".

Since Prohibition was law during the heyday of the Dill Pickle Club, the main room at No. 10 Tooker Alley was called the Tea Room. According to their literary magazine, The Dill Pickler, which was printed here, the purpose of the club was as follows: *"The Dill Pickle Club is chartered in the State of Illinois as a Non-Profit Organization for the promotion of the Arts, Crafts, Literature, and Science."*

The club was raided twice during the 1920's when the police tried to prevent freedom of speech at the club, but the members successfully got an injunction against the police.

One of the plays first presented in their theatre was "Winesburg, Ohio" by Sherwood Anderson.

It was here that Carl Sandburg first read many of his poems about Chicago.

Ben Hecht, an active member of the club, wrote in his, "The Voice of Labor", something that is still true today:

"You'll hear no sound of the forge, you'll hear no ringing of the hammar, no echo of the grunt of men lifting stone, shaping wood, and swinging picks at the earth. This silence is the history of labor. The history of labor is an epic of silence."

Jack Jones, known as "The Manager" of the club, was a member of the Painters' Union as well as an auto repairman. Jones once described the club as a meeting place for "Irish revolutionists, labor leaders, artists, sculptors, poets, writers, and assorted nuts." It must have been an exciting place!

By the 1950's the Dill Pickle Club was gone but the College of Complexes carried on its tradition from a storefront on State Street about one block west. Today the College of Complexes still meets every Saturday night in an old hotel on Clark Street.

36. WASHINGTON SQUARE (Between Delaware and Walton along Dearborn Street)

The park area on your left is known to Chicagoans as "Bughouse Square". This park was originally deeded to the city in 1842 by a land dealer named Orasmus Bushnell. Since the surrounding area was then wealthy estates and townhouses, the park was largely for the local residents until the turn of the century. However by 1900, this neighborhood was becoming the Greenwich Village of Chicago, and Washington Square was Chicago's Hyde Park Corner. The area became known as "The Village" or "Towertown", and this square rang with soapbox oratory, political controversy, and religious fervor.

Lucy Parsons was prevented from speaking here by the police in 1909, but eventually "free speech" in Chicago and "Bughouse Square" became synonomous.

A speaker in "Bughouse Square" had to be adept at holding a crowd as well as handling hecklers, who were often as good as the speakers. Such celebrated speakers as Clarence Darrow, Ben Hecht, Carl Sandburg, and Emma Goldman once spoke in this square. William Lloyd (Bill) Smith, known as the "King of the Soap-Box", spoke here many times, and later founded the College of Complexes.

The favorite topics and regular speakers shifted with the decades. In the 1920's, Prohibition was often the subject debated. In the 1930's, everyone proposed solutions to the Great Depression. Then pacifists and others debated World War II in the early 1940's. In the 1950's, not even McCarthyism and the activities of J. Edgar Hoover could shut off debate; but the rise of television and the movement of the Bohemian type neighborhoods toward Old Town and New Town further north brought an end to oratory in "Bughouse Square".

However, on May 2, 1975, the third anniversary of the death of J. Edgar Hoover, a loosely affiliated alliance of many individuals and groups in Chicago formed the Committee to Re-Open Bughouse Square; and for one evening "Bughouse Square" was again filled with people and debate as it was in the past.

Facing the square is the Newberry Library, which has material on labor in its collections.

37. FORMER SITE OF NORTHSIDE TURNER HALL
(Formerly near northwest corner of Clark and Division Street)

Turn left on to Division Street and go west one block to Clark; turn north on Clark. As you turn the corner of Clark and Division you are passing the former site of the Northside Turner Hall. This was once a working class neighborhood of Germans, Swedes, and many other ethnic groups. In the 1950's this area was almost completely leveled, an area of over eight city blocks.

The Northside Turner Hall that served the German workers in this neighborhood was like the 27 other Turner Halls that existed in Chicago at the turn of the century. It had a beer garden, gymnasiums, meeting rooms, and music rooms. These halls were often raided by the police. The Northside Turner Hall was regularly used by Spies and other socialist groups. As late as the 1920's there was a book store here, and the Dill Pickler Magazine carried the following announcement in 1924:

"Under the wing of the North Side Turner Hall, the Radical Book Shop has a display of literature, radical and conservative and is now featuring a sale of the old Kerr publications."

38. CARL SANDBURG VILLAGE (Along Clark Street between Division and North Avenue)

As you drive along Clark Street you will see on both sides of you new high rises and townhouses that make up the complex known as Carl Sandburg Village. This was originally supposed to be the "Fort Dearborn Project", which was to be low income housing for Chicago workers. Instead the realtor, Arthur Rubloff, built upper middle income housing which appeals to young single men and women who work in the loop.

Carl Sandburg, "The Poet of the People", would be horrified to have this area named after him. Individual buildings are named after other famous American writers and poets.

39. GERMANIA CLUB (Northwest corner of Clark and Germania Place)

The Germania Club was founded in 1864 and has occupied this building since the 1880's. Attempts were made to tear down the Germania Club, but this beautiful building was saved.

Governor Altgeld was a member and his portrait is in an honored place in the second floor dining room. This building was a center for music, lectures and dances. It would be the musical Germans of Chicago who would support another German, Theodore Thomas, the founder of the Chicago Symphony Orchestra.

40. CHICAGO HISTORICAL SOCIETY (Northeast corner of Clark and North Avenue in Lincoln Park)

This museum has many displays on the history of the city and a wonderful library that contains materials dealing with Haymarket. The library also has a fine collection of papers and letters of labor leaders, including the papers of John Fitzpatrick, former President of the Chicago Federation of Labor, A. Phillip Randolph, Mary McDowell, and the Chicago Teachers Union.

41. MOODY CHURCH (Near Northwest corner of Clark and North Avenue)

Across from the Chicago Historical Society are a group of unusual red brick buildings which house the Moody Church.

This church was founded by Dwight L. Moody, who first came to Chicago in 1856. Moody worked among the poor and uneducated of the city. By 1873, Moody had teamed up with another evangelist named Sankey, and they erected a great tabernacle on Monroe Street between Franklin and Wacker Drive which would hold over 8000 people. This tabernacle was used by Moody during the Railroad Strike of 1877 to hold prayer meetings. Moody believed that the poor should not demonstrate and that they should suffer on earth and find salvation in heaven. Moody received large donations from many of the wealthy businessmen of the city, who probably saw his philosophy as beneficial to their interests. One of the largest contributors would be Victor Lawson (See No. 32).

Moody's ideas were not far from those of Rev. Henry Ward Beecher of Boston who incurred the wrath of workers throughout America when he said during the Railroad Strike of 1877 that workers didn't need more money since water was free and bread was cheap and that was all that a worker needed to sustain life.

Samuel Fielden, who was a Methodist lay preacher himself, heard Dwight Moody and went up to talk to him in the tabernacle after his lecture. This talk resulted in the beginning of a debate between the two men. Fielden, like Dr. Martin Luther King, believed that workers should fight for better wages and living conditions.

Fielden went to Joliet Prison for his ideas, and Dr. King would be assassinated while helping the striking municipal workers of Memphis, Tennessee.

Today the Moody Church operates radio station WMBI, as well as the Moody Bible Institute on LaSalle Street and Chicago Avenue.

42. SCHILLER STATUE (In Lincoln Park near Stockton and Webster)

Although not directly on the tour route, you may wish to see this statue of the writer Schiller, who lived from 1759-1805, and was greatly admired by the German workers who settled in Chicago.

This statue played a part in the Haymarket Affair, since the Chicago Police and State's Attorney Grinnell claimed that on the evening of May 4, 1886 the German workers had planned to gather around this statue before beginning the revolutionary take over of the city and the bombings of the homes of the rich.

The statue, modeled after one in Marbach, Germany, is by the Chicago sculptor, Ernst Raus. The statue wasn't even completed on May 4 when the police claimed the workers were going to gather here, but it was officially unveiled on May 8, 1886 by a group known as the Chicago Citizens of German Descent. This statue was a source of great pride to the German community that had been discriminated against since their arrival in Chicago in the late 1840's.

43. THE SECOND CITY THEATRE (Near Northwest corner of North Avenue and Wells, 1616 N. Wells)

Turning left off Clark Street at North Avenue you begin to pass through the heart of what was once the old north side German community.

At the northwest corner of North and Wells is Piper's Alley, formerly a German bakery. Directly north of Piper's Alley is the Theatre of the Second City Company.

This theatre is decorated with ornamentation from the old Schiller Theatre which originally stood at 64 W. Randolph and was designed by the great American architect, Louis Sullivan. This ornamentation contains the faces of German writers, poets, musicians, and liberal political leaders that were admired by the German workers. German young people didn't even hear about many of their national heroes in Chicago schools since bi-lingual and cultural education was not allowed until the administration of Governor Altgeld.

The Schiller Theatre was later renamed the Garrick Theatre, since anti-German feeling was strong in Chicago during World War I. It was here that Rev. Carwardine spoke at the time of the Pullman Strike of 1894, asking for relief and food for the starving people of Pullman.

The Schiller Theatre was also the scene of a weekly lecture series conducted by the Workers' University Society. Among the speakers in this series was Clarence Darrow who debated in 1916 with Professor Scott Nearing on the theme "Will Democracy Cure the Social Ills of the World?" Jack London, Jane Addams, and many others spoke there.

It is sad that this once beautiful theatre is gone and that only this ornamentation from the entrance remains, but the Second City Company performs here the kind of social parody of society that the Haymarket Martyrs might have enjoyed.

44. FORMER SITE OF MUELLER'S HALL (Between North Park Avenue and Sedgwick on the northside of the street)

You are now passing through the area where many of the Haymarket Martyrs lived. A large new apartment building at

300 North Avenue stands on the block once occupied by Mueller Hall.

Here on January 12, 1885, a meeting was held at which the police claimed that Albert Parsons advocated the use of bombs and the overthrow of American society. Captain Schaack sent a police spy to the meeting by the name of Michael Hoffman. Officer Hoffman, disguised as a workman, reported that Parsons said the following:

"Gentlemen, before we call this meeting to order . . . I want you to see if there are any reporters or policemen present. See if you can discover any spies. If you find any one here, you can do with him as you please, but my advice to you is, take him and strangle him and then throw him out of the window: then let the people think that the fellow fell out. And if you should give one of them a chance for his life, tell him, if he has any more notions to come to our meetings, he should first go to St. Michael's Church (See No. 47), see the priest and prepare to die, say farewell to all his friends and family . . . and then let him enter."

Since Officer Hoffman lived to report the meeting, Parsons alleged threat was not carried out.

In early 1975 many community groups found out that police spying of this kind was still going on in Chicago.

Mueller Hall was also the scene for the funeral of Meta Neebe, the first wife of Oscar Neebe. Meta and Oscar Neebe lived on Sedgwick just off North Avenue around the corner from this hall. The long trial affected Meta's health and she died on March 11, 1887. A great funeral was planned for Mueller Hall and they hoped for over 20,000 people. Actually less than 2,000 attended, probably because Meta was not connected actively with the labor movement. However, Lucy Parsons, Nina Van Zandt Spies, and the three trial attorneys came.

Neebe was released from Joliet Prison for the funeral and held in the Cook County Jail. He attended part of the service, but he was advised by the State's Attorney not to go to the burial, since this could prejudice a future appeal he might make for his release. The State's Attorney feared the burial might create a riot of some kind, especially with Neebe there.

45. FORMER SITE OF SELIGER-LINGG RESIDENCE
(Near Southwest Corner of North and Sedgwick, 1544 Sedgwick)

Just south of North Avenue on Sedgwick, under the elevated, is a business building that occupies the former site of the home of Mr. and Mrs. Seliger.

Originally two houses occupied this lot. At the front was a three story building and at the back was a small structure where Lingg had his room.

Long before Lingg rented space, William Seliger had been making bombs in the rear building, yet Seliger would turn State's witness and Lingg would be given the death penalty.

Lingg had only come to America the year before in order to escape the military draft in Germany. Lingg had no relatives or friends in Chicago, but he did have his sweetheart, Ida Miller, who supported him to the end. Lingg was strikingly good-looking and the Chicago papers wrote many stories about him, including one that he was the illegitimate son of a German nobleman.

During Lingg's short time in Chicago, he had refused to become a strikebreaker during a carpenters' strike, and was blacklisted. He then became involved in the Trades and Labor Assembly of the city. Lingg was at the McCormick Plant on May 3rd listening to August Spies when Inspector Bonfield and the police came. Lingg was one of those clubbed.

Seliger testified that he and Lingg made a number of bombs on the afternoon of May 4th, which Lingg wished delivered to Neff's Hall (See No. 50) where, according to Seliger, radicals were supposed to pick them up. These bombs were then to be used to blow up police stations and businesses throughout the city.

When the police raids took place under orders from Captain Schaack, this bomb factory was found and Seliger and his wife were arrested. Lingg was found several days later in the Pilsen neighborhood where he was hiding in the home of a Jewish family.

One of the curiosities of the Haymarket Affair is the fact that the Seligers were not tried. Their expenses were paid by the police, and eventually they were given a trip back to Germany where they died. In Captain Schaack's book Mr. and Mrs. Seliger were presented as heroes and brave witnesses.

46. BUILDINGS SIMILAR TO SELIGER-LINGG RESIDENCE (1547 Hudson Avenue)

Although not visible from your car, directly behind the former site of the Seliger-Lingg residence are two interesting structures. By looking at the house on Hudson Street and the building behind, you can see what the Seliger house and so-called "bomb factory" looked like in 1886. Two houses on one lot was typical at that time. German working class families that lived in this neighborhood in the 1880's needed the extra income and built and rented as much space as they could. The area was very densely populated.

47. ST. MICHAEL'S CHURCH AND SCHOOL (Northside of North Avenue at Cleveland Street)

Continuing westward on North Avenue you will see on your right the spire of old St. Michael's Church with its beautiful clock tower. This is the oldest German Catholic church in the city and is the church that Parsons referred to in his speech at Mueller's Hall.

This church was founded in 1852 by the Very Reverend Anthony Kapp, then vicar-general for the Chicago German Catholic Community. This beautiful church building, a very large edifice in the Romanesque style, was built in 1866. It has the distinction of being one of the few buildings to have survived the Chicago Fire of 1871.

Captain Schaack and the newspapers claimed that the anarchists were planning to blow up this church as a part of the so-called "Haymarket Uprisings". There is absolutely no proof that anything like this was planned, but stories of this kind probably helped to alienate the more conservative and religious members of the German community from the cause of the workers.

In the 1920's St. Michael's School was the largest Catholic school in the city with over 1,700 children in attendance. Today, as a result of urban renewal many of the German families who had lived here for generations have left.

48. HOME OF ALBERT AND LUCY PARSONS IN 1879
(1908 Mohawk Street)

Although not on the tour route you may wish to turn off North Avenue at Mohawk and drive north three blocks to a well-preserved house near the northwest corner of Mohawk and Menomonee Streets.

The Parsons moved many times and this is one of four of their homes which is still standing. It was to this neighborhood that Albert Parsons first came to live when he came to Chicago in 1873 from Waco, Texas. He had worked as a printer for his brother in Texas, and he became a printer and a founder of the Typographical Workers Union in Chicago, Local 1307 of the Knights of Labor.

Albert came to Chicago with his beautiful black wife, Lucy, who spoke Spanish and was also of Indian blood. Her maiden name was Gathing, and she had probably been a slave prior to the Civil War. They could not live together in Texas as man and wife, since mixed marriages were outlawed. They came to Chicago to find a better life, but, unfortunately, they found prejudice and injustice here as well.

Their only son, Albert R. Parsons Jr., was born in this house on September 14, 1879. The midwife recorded on the birth certificate under "Race or Color" the word "Nigger" in describing the new baby.

The young Albert at 14 on June 25, 1893 would pull the string to unveil the Martyrs' Monument in Waldheim Cemetery (See No. 99). However, Albert Jr. would have a tragic life, as did all members of the Parsons family. At the age of 19 he contracted tuberculosis and he had serious mental problems, probably as a result of all the tragedy during his childhood. He spent the rest of his life in the Elgin Sanatorium and died there in 1919.

49. FORMER SITE OF THE HOME OF ALBERT AND LUCY PARSONS IN 1877 (1901 Larrabee Street)

This site is off the tour route and there is little to see today, since most of the old dwellings along Larrabee have been leveled. A new townhouse now has the number 1901. One older home of the 1880's is still standing, however, directly north of the former site of the Parsons' house, giving you some idea of what this street once looked like. Parsons lived here at the time of the Great Railroad Strike when he was "black-listed" by the Times.

50. FORMER SITE OF THE HOME OF ALBERT AND LUCY PARSONS IN 1881 (1656 Larrabee Street)

This site is off the tour route. Only a vacant lot between two very old frame buildings marks the spot where the Parsons lived when their daughter Lulu was born on April 20, 1881.

Lulu, a beautiful child, was only six years old when her father was executed. Three years after the execution she died of a rare bone disease, having been in terrible pain for several years. Union newspapers throughout the country printed stories of sympathy to Lucy Parsons, whose life seemed to be filled with one tragedy after another.

51. FORMER SITE OF THE LARRABEE POLICE STATION (Corner of North Avenue and Larrabee)

Although demolished many years ago, the Larrabee Police Station (sometimes called the North Avenue Station) played a part in the Haymarket Trial.

The Larrabee Police Station

According to the testimony of William Seliger against Lingg, they had carried a large trunk up North Avenue with each of them holding one end. This trunk was filled with bombs they had made in the so-called "Bomb Factory". Seliger testified that upon reaching this police station, Lingg suggested throwing a bomb through the window; but Seliger said he talked Lingg out of doing this and saved the lives of the men in the station.

According to Captain Schaack and his "Haymarket Uprising" theory, this was one of the many stations to be bombed in the worker takeover of Chicago. General Trumbull, the distinguished attorney and friend of Abraham Lincoln, thought this was ridiculous and wrote the following:

"The conspiracy which the prosecution attempted to show at the trial, and which it pretended they did show, was not carried into execution in any of its essential details.

As illustrated and explained by the Supreme Court itself, it was a conspiracy that aimed at a social and political revolution.

Hundreds, aye, thousands of men were engaged in it. It was to begin by the throwing of bombs into the North Avenue station and into other stations in the city. Well-drilled men, armed with rifles, were to be stationed outside to shoot the police as they came out; then the conspirators were to march inward, toward the heart of the city, destroying whatever should oppose them; the telegraph wires and the hose of the firemen would be cut, and the reign of Anarchy begin.

Nothing of the kind occurred; nothing of it was attempted; nothing of it prepared for, except the making of bombs by Lingg."

52. CLYBOURN AND NORTH AVENUE BEER HALLS

Continuing westward on North Avenue, we come to Clybourn Avenue which crosses at an angle. Clybourn Avenue was one of the early "plank roads" that ran in a northwesterly direction out of the city along the eastside of the Chicago River.

Michael Schwab, who never attended the Haymarket meeting but was given a life sentence anyway, was speaking that night to a rally at the Deering Harvester Plant which was then located on Clybourn Avenue.

Clybourn Avenue and the sidestreets in this area were once filled with German, Bohemian, and Scandinavian beer halls and meeting rooms. There were several cooperative beer halls that sold beer to the workers at reduced prices.

Neff's Hall where Lingg is suppose to have taken the bombs

The only German business left today is the Golden Ox Restaurant which can be seen on your left. Sieben's Beer Gardens was an institution here for generations, but it was closed and demolished in the 1960's.

Several beer halls in this area played a part in the Haymarket Affair. It was at Neff's Hall that Lingg and Seliger were supposed to have left the bombs after carrying them all the way from their home on Sedgwick.

This is what came out of Seliger's testimony:

"At about eight-thirty in the evening, Lingg and Seliger left the

house. They carried between them, by means of a stick through the handle, a small trunk filled with these bombs. The trunk weighed some thirty to fifty pounds . . . That is the way we were carrying the trunk which was taken to Neff's Hall . . . We took the package into the building, and through the saloon on the side into the hallway that led to the rear. After the bombs were put down in the passageway, there were different ones there, three or four, who took bombs out for themselves!

Also in this area was Liberty Hall (also known as Bohemia Hall). Supposedly a meeting was held here on May 2, 1886 at 10:30 p.m. George Engel is supposed to have proposed the "Haymarket Uprising" or "Conspiracy Plan" here according to Captain Schaack.

53. OLD CHICAGO BEER (Northwest corner of North Avenue and Sheffield)

As you drive through this area you pass dozens of small factories that line both sides of the street in this old industrial district that once employed many of the immigrant German, Polish, Irish, and Scandinavian workers of the city.

At the corner of North and Sheffield is Chicago's last home brewery. In a city that was once filled with brewers, the former Peter-Hand Brewery, which now makes Old Chicago beer, is the last.

The business leaders of the city did not like beer or beer halls. The beer halls were the meeting places of the workers on their one and only day off, Sunday. The police claimed that in the beer halls the workers were plotting the overthrow of the "Establishment" of the city. The police enforced Sunday closing laws and they often used the liquor licensing laws to prevent freedom of speech and assembly.

Lucy Parsons was speaking one Sunday in a hall, and the police used the liquor laws to arrest her and put her in jail. The police were upset when they found that the hall had not served liquor and they had to release Lucy.

Oscar Neebe's business was selling yeast to the brewers of the city, and Neebe founded the Beer Wagon Drivers Union in Chicago, which was the beginning of the Teamsters Union.

54. VIEW OF GOOSE ISLAND, EARLY INDUSTRIAL AREAS, AND ST. STANISLAS CHURCH (North Avenue Bridge over the Chicago River)

You may want to park your car for a short time and look at this very different view of the City of Chicago. This is not the Lake Shore Drive view that appears on postcards, but this is the view that the ethnic workers of the city saw.

From the North Avenue bridge over the Chicago River you can see the skyline of the city to the southeast, and directly in front of you is the northern end of Goose Island. This area became an island when deep channels were cut through this area of the Chicago River so that large ships could go through.

Harvey Zorbaugh, a writer, described this area in 1929:

"A great deal of shipping once went up the river, and tugs, coal barges, tramp freighters and occasional ore boats still whistle at its bridges and steam slowly around its bends. This shipping caused commerce and industry to locate along the river, and today wharves, lumber and coal yards, iron works, gas works, sheet metal works, light manufacturing plants and storage plants, wholesale houses for spices, furs, groceries, butter, and

imported oils line both sides of the river for miles, and with the noise and smoke of the railroads make a great barrier that half encircles the Near North Side, renders the part of it along the river undesirable to live . . . . "

Because of the pollution from the factories the area was known as "Smoky Hollow".

Looking to the southwest one sees the beautiful green tower of St. Stanislaus Church. It is difficult to imagine how this area looked in the 1850's when the first Polish immigrant workers settled here. Instead of industry this entire area was swamp and a vast prairie along the edges of the Chicago River.

Between the 1850's and the 1870's the early Polish settlement here was served by a Polish missionary named Father Leopold Moczygemba, who made his annual visit each Easter time to administer to the Polish Catholics. In the early months of 1866, the Poles formed the Society of St. Stanislaus, and in 1867 a total of 150 Polish families asked the Bishop of Chicago, Thomas Foley, who was Irish, for permission to form the first Polish parish in the city.

Although St. Stanislaus is not directly on the tour route you may wish to see it at some other time. It is located at Nobel and Evergreen in the heart of "Old Chicago Polonia". The first church for the community was a simple frame building, but the present beautiful Roman basilica type church was built in 1875. It is 200 feet long and 80 feet wide. There were once two towers (one has been removed). Between the towers is a giant 17 foot statue of St. Stanislaus. The church will hold 1,500 people, but at one time as many as 18,000 people would come to Easter services and many couldn't even get near the church.

Under the leadership of Father Michael Barzynski beginning in the 1880's this church became involved in social action including a newspaper, a museum, and an insurance company. Father Barzynski inspired a local Polish girl to become a nun, and as Sister Theresa she founded a new order to help the people of the community. Sister Theresa may soon be declared a saint by the Catholic Church. The life of Chicago Poles was one of great poverty and persecution for many years. Today there are over 900,000 people of Polish ancestry living in the Chicago Metropolitan Area, and the majority of them can trace their roots back to this area.

55. NORTH AVENUE, MILWAUKEE, AND DAMEN BUSINESS AREA

Proceeding westward along North Avenue, you pass more small factories on the west side of the Chicago River. You will also notice old homes built at the old land level before the streets were raised in the 1860's and 1870's; small bridges have been built from the sidewalk to the second floor to provide entrance into the buildings.

At the busy intersection of North, Milwaukee, and Damen we enter the area known as West Town or Wicker Park. This area was the very edge of the city in the 1880's.

The first settlers here were Germans who wished to escape the German ghetto that is now Chicago's Old Town area. Many Scandinavians who worked in the lumberyards that lined the river also came to live here. By 1910, the Polish population was increasing and Russian Jews and Italians came to live in the area. In the 1930's some Blacks moved into the area, but the great change came in the 1960's when Puerto Ricans became the largest single group. Many Serbs and Ukranians also found homes here, and many still live in this neighborhood.

56. ASSOCIATION HOUSE (2150 W. North Avenue)

A few blocks further west on North Avenue we pass Association House, a settlement house which has served this area for over three-quarters of a century.

In June of 1899, an estimated 1,500 girls and women living in West Town worked in the tailor shops, laundries, factories, and in other business in the area. There were numerous saloon-dance halls, but few other recreational facilities. Miss Susan Poxon, a city missionary for the Moody Church, appealed to the Young Women's Christian Association for funds to set up a settlement house for women.

In 1900, when boys and men were admitted to the program, the YWCA decided not to support the program anymore. The YWCA had never liked the idea of having a "settlement house"; so very early the name "Association House" was used instead of Young Women's Christian Association House. After the YWCA dropped their support, a board of directors of businessmen in the Wicker Park Area was set up and Northwestern University and several suburban communities began to contribute staff and funds. The corner stone of this building at 2150 W. North Avenue was laid by Jane Addams on September 9, 1905. This building, like Hull House, served the needs of the surrounding community. Women's clubs, men's clubs, educational classes, even a summer camp at Druce Lake were provided by Association House. In the 1920's there was a nutrition clinic for the children of the neighborhood. An Infant Welfare Society existed from 1921 until the middle of 1970.

During the Depression of the 1930's, Association House gave emergency aid to the starving people of the neighborhood until Roosevelt's New Deal aid programs finally took over.

When rioting broke out within the Puerto Rican community, in June, 1966, Association House set up the "Puerto Rican Cultural Club" to give the young people of the community a pride in their language, culture, and heritage.

Association House is having financial difficulties today, but it is trying to continue to serve this community.

NOTE: After turning left at Leavitt Street and left again at Pierce, park your car and walk from sites 57 to 60.

57. BOUMENOT, HORN, AND BIELECKI HOUSES (2156, 2150, and 2146 Pierce Street)

Many wealthy German businessmen lived in the Wicker Park area. These German business leaders were not accepted in the wealthy areas of the Gold Coast which were reserved for the Anglo-Saxon Protestant "Establishment" of the city.

The German businessmen wished to show off their wealth and they built some beautiful and unique homes here. Let us hope that the charm of this area will be preserved for the enjoyment of future generations.

The Germans in this neighborhood were in the hotel and restaurant businesses, banking, and meat packing, as well as lumber and the manufacture of beer. The Scandinavian carpenters and cabinetmakers who lived in the more modest surrounding homes were responsible for the beautiful woodwork you'll see on many of the homes in Wicker Park.

With the installation of streetcar lines during the 1890's, and the completion of the Logan Square and Humbolt branches of the elevated lines in 1895, this area boomed. As the German businessmen moved further out in the country, Polish workers took advantage of the cheap transportation in the area, bought up these mansions, and turned them into rooming houses.

The Boumenot House at 2156 as well as the two houses to the east were obviously designed by the same architect in the early 1890's. They were meant to be more impressive from the front than from the sides or back in order to show off the owners' newly acquired wealth.

The Boumenot House is built of brick and red sandstone. The front of the house is in the popular and impressive, Romanesque Style of the 1890's while the sides of the house are in the more modest Queen Anne Style that had been popular in the 1880's.

Notice how the castle-like roof and the carved front were designed to impress the viewer.

John and Mary Boumenot purchased this house in 1974 for only $16,000, and they have spent a great deal of money turning this former boarding house into a beautiful home again. The first floor is still a rental unit, but the Boumenots have extensively renovated the second and third floors. The Boumenots are typical of the young people who are now moving into this area.

The J.B. Horn House at 2150 Pierce is more elaborate than its neighbors to the east and west. It is built of gray limestone with a very impressive front porch supported by marble columns. The carriage stone near the curb by the driveway has the name J.B. Horn on it, and we must assume he was one of the early owners.

This house is now owned by friends of the Boumenot family. Many of the beautiful iron fences of Wicker Park remain, but they have now been supplemented by high stockade type fences. The newer more affluent residents, the poorer newly arrived minority groups, and the older residents of this area do not always see eye to eye on the future development of Wicker Park. It will be interesting to see if it is possible here to bring about "urban renewal and restoration" without driving out the workers and older citizens of this community. This will require a great deal of cooperation and understanding.

The Bieleck House at 2146 has been owned by this family for many years. It is built of red sandstone like the Boumenot House and some of the original iron fencing remains in the front. The number "85" appears in stained glass over the front door, since this was its number before the new city-wide system was adopted in 1909. This house is slightly different from the others along the east side which faces a beautiful old red brick alley.

NOTE: Although this tour does not include **Caton Street,** if you are particularly interested in the architecture of this area you may wish to walk three blocks north along Leavitt to the 2100 block of Caton Street. This is one of the most beautifully restored blocks in Wicker Park, containing old German burgher houses, many with great ball rooms on the third floors.

58. PADEREWSKI HOUSE (2138 Pierce)

This fascinating home is known as the Paderewski House because the great Polish pianist and statesman, Ignace Paderewski played a piano concert on the front porch in the early 1930's. At this time the building was being used as the Polish Consulate in Chicago. The entire street was closed off, and thousands of people came to hear Paderewski play. A short time after this Paderewski was elected President of Poland. It was he more than any other who had fought for Poland's right to self-determination after W.W.I. and at the time of the Conference at Versailles. The Polish Museum (See No. 75) has a great deal of material on this man who was greatly loved by Polish workers both in Poland and America.

The architectural style of this house is beyond description, but perhaps "Swiss Chalet" or "Viennese Cottage Style" can best describe it. The original builder was probably German. The front porches and the Greek styled westside bay window are later additions.

The beautiful carved woodwork of the outside is also continued throughout the inside of the house, and the year of 1882 is carved into the dark woodwork of the front hall stairway. Also, in the front hall is a beautiful stained glass window to Queen Hedwig, the ruler of Poland when the country was larger than all of Western Europe. This stained glass window on the east side of the house was probably added when the house was the Polish consulate since several lines of Polish writing appear on the window.

The beautiful stained glass windows you see from the outside of the house are of particular interest, especially the rose windows on the doors going out to the third story balcony. These windows and the others in the front were probably added around 1910.

The beautiful iron fence which surrounds this house also surrounds the Noel House to the east, testifying to the fact that more lawn and garden area once surrounded it.

At the time of the stock market crash of 1929, the house was owned by a prominent banker named Jan Smulski, who owned a bank at Ashland and Division Streets. Like so many immigrants he had worked hard to become rich, but with the crash he lost everything. This together with the fact that he found he had cancer, caused him to commit suicide here.

This house has been owned for many years by the Lukowich family. Although it is now broken into many apartments, the appearance is still that of a single family dwelling. The old carriage house at the back is also divided into apartments.

59. KRAMPS HOUSE (2137 Pierce) AND THE JERGENS HOUSE (2141 Pierce)

The Kramps family still lives in this house, built for them some time in the 1880's. Although the style is a variation of the "Queen Anne Style" that was popular at this time, unusual things have been done with the carved wood balcony on the eastside of the building, and the beautiful use of both wood and metal under the roof at the front of the building.

Notice the way the German artisans combined the red brick, limestone, and unusual green stone around the big picture window to create a very pleasing affect. A kind of "fish-tail" design" divides the panels of the front window. Look particularly at the stained glass over both the first and second floor picture windows.

For several generations the Kramps were doctors in the area, and there is a Kramps' Chapel at St. Elizabeth Hospital named after the family. Marie Kramps still lives in this house.

The Jergens House to the west of the Kramps House is probably from the early 1890's. The old number "82" appears in the stainedglass over the doorway, and limestone gargoyles look down from near the top of the front of the house.

The Jergens family was originally in the tire manufacturing business, and they sold the house in the early 1950's and moved to Oak Park, Illinois. From 1954 to 1971 the house was the home of the Ukranian Archbishop of the Russian Orthodox Holy Virgin Protection Church. The cross is still to be seen at the top of the building.

The style of the Jergens House is "Romanesque" in the front, but the sides are in the earlier "Queen Anne Style". On the east side of the house facing the garden is a first floor conservatory with sleeping rooms above. There was no air conditioning in the 1890's, not even for the rich.

The third floor has a finished attic which was used as a ballroom. Many of the German families and later the Poles used these third floor rooms for musical concerts as well as dances.

Although there were once many stained glass windows in this house, most of them have been replaced with glass brick. One of the windows still in the house is a portrait in glass of the then Princess of Prussia. A few of the old stained glass windows may still be seen from the alley along the west side of the house.

60. THE J.R. NOEL HOUSE (2134 Pierce)

This house was built in 1903 for the president of a local bank, J.R. Noel, who was a Board Member of Association House (See No. 56). The house was sold after his death to a number of owners, but it was finally purchased by Association House in October of 1940 and became known as "The Residence". Later it was again sold to private owners.

This house is in the "Neo-Classical Style" and was probably built by the same architect who designed the house two door east at 2118 Pierce. The Noel House has a beautiful stained glass window next to the main entrance. The house is built of buff-colored brick with cut gray limestone decorating the front. The house now belongs to the Vaughan family.

The house directly to the east 2124 Pierce is much older than the Noel house and probably dates from the 1880's. A porch which once decorated the east half of the front of the house has been removed.

The house at 2118, is similar to the Noel House and has basically the same floor plan, but is in the "French Chateau Style".

NOTE: Return to your car and drive from No. 61 to 66, where you may wish to view some additional homes on foot.

61. WICKER PARK (East side of Damen between N. Wicker Park Blvd. and Schiller)

After driving along Pierce to Damen, turn right and you will see Wicker Park on your left. This four acre wedge of greenery was donated by Isham Wicker, a 19th century Chicago developer. He donated the park land to enhance the homesites in this area when the region was being developed in the 1870's and 1880's.

Edgar Lee Master in his book "Tales of Chicago" wrote about Wicker Park:

"Around the corner from Milwaukee Avenue on Robey Street (now Damen) was Wicker Park, and off that many streets where German politicians and manufacturers and packers lived in houses of brick or stone enjoying comfortable fortunes of a hundred thousand or so. There was a tendency here to adopt architecture for comparatively small houses which made them mansions on a small scale."

According to State's Attorney Grinnell in his opening address at the Haymarket Trial on July 15, 1886, this park was to be the site for the beginning of the anarchist take-over of Chicago. Grinnell said:

". . . Lingg went around with bombs in his pocket that night and desired to throw them at a patrol wagon and was only restrained by his friends. And they were to build a fire up toward Wicker Park . . . some building was to be set on fire for the purpose of attracting the police in that direction . . . . "

The police also believed that bombs were buried under the park, and so in the days after the Haymarket bombing the park was dug up; but no bombs were found.

68. TOWNHOUSES FACING WICKER PARK (1900 Block of Schiller)

The Flores House at 1941 Schiller is a fortress-like structure built of limestone in the front and brick on the sides. The Flores family are active with Wicker Park community groups and have done a great deal of work to this beautiful mansion. The iron fence around the building formerly surrounded the playground of one of Chicago's old public schools.

The Quales House at 1951 Schiller was built before 1876 by Niles T. Quales when Schiller Street was still Fowler Street. When Germans moved into this neighborhood they petitioned to have many of the streets renamed for people who meant something to them. The Quales Houses has a window with an unusual shape on the second floor.

63. HOME OF THE SPIES FAMILY (2132 Potomac)

After driving two blocks past Wicker Park, turn right onto Potomac Street. At 2132 Potomac you will find the home of August Spies. Spies lived here with his mother, three younger brothers and his sister, and he helped to support all of them.

August Spies was born in Landeck in Central Germany. He was perhaps the best educated of the Haymarket Martyrs and he spoke several languages. Spies believed his philosophy for social change would bring an industrial Reformation, and he thought of Bonfield, Grinnell, Pinkerton, and Chicago's businessmen as belonging to the Dark Ages.

Spies' father died when he was only seventeen, and Spies as the oldest took over as head of the house. He decided to come to America in 1872 and landed in New York. He traveled throughout the South, worked on a farm, and even went on an expedition into Upper Canada. Then in 1873 he came to Chicago, where he went into the upholstery business for the next six years finally setting up his own shop in 1876. When he could afford it he brought his family to America, and they moved to this house in Wicker Park.

Spies became active in the cause of Chicago workers. As early as 1875 he was attending socialist lectures. He was shocked by the use of Federal troops against workers during the Railroad Strike of 1877, and decided to get involved in politics. In 1877 he joined the Socialist-Labor Party. Spies first got into trouble with the police at the Chicago Avenue Police Station when he reported to the authorities the brutality of a desk sergeant there toward a young girl named Martha Seidel.

Spies was handsome, well-dressed, and an excellent speaker. The Democratic Party in 1884 were so fearful of his speeches against Grover Cleveland that a banker, E.S. Dreyer, offered Spies $10,000 to stop saying damaging things about Cleveland to the workers. Spies refused, and even began an investigation of Mr. Dreyer.

Spies was a delegate to the Socialist Convention in Chicago in 1881, a delegate to the International Workingmen's Party of America Convention in Pittsburgh in 1883, and worked with the 4,000 striking miners of the Hocking Valley Strike of 1884-85. Spies liked to dress up and go downtown to dinner in the finer restaurants frequented by the "Establishment" of the city, and this made many of the businessmen angry. Spies was also a member of Ameri-Kanische Turner Bund, one of the Turner Clubs. By the time of the Haymarket Affair, Spies had been editor of the German language worker paper, the Arbeiter-Zeitung, for several years.

After the execution of the Haymarket Martyrs, each of the bodies was returned to their families with the exception of Lingg who had no family in America; his body was turned over to the Engel family. It was to this house that Spies' body was taken, and it was placed on view here on Saturday, November 12, 1887. The Daily News described the scene at this house on that Saturday so many years ago:

The Spies home in 1887

" . . . *Long strips of white and black crepe swung from the doorbell. At the top of the symbols of mourning was a large black rose, made also of crepe, and from the middle of the rose streamers of red fluttered in the breeze . . . .*

From the moment the dead body arrived at the residence . . . the house had been surrounded by crowds of inquisitive spectators. This morning the assembliage gradually increased in numbers all anxious to get a look at the face of the famous anarchist . . . . "

The Daily News told what occured to one of their reporters when he met August Spies' brother, Chris, in front of the house on Saturday, November 12th:

"A photographer called about noon and took a picture of the surroundings. As his cab bowled away a brother of August suddenly made his appearance in the throng of people before the door. His eyes were red and grief, in unmistakable lines, was written on his rugged countenance. A sharp, searching glance over the crowd revealed to the man the presence of a Daily News reporter.

'I will have nothing to do with the Daily News. The paper hunted August to his grave, and the sooner you get out of here the better!' exclaimed the irate brother."

The funeral was to be held on Sunday, November 13, and the plan was for the procession to start here at the Spies House and then to go along Milwaukee Avenue by the homes of the other Haymarket Martyrs picking up another body at each stop. Then the procession would procede into the Loop and by train out to the cemetery. *This is the general route we will follow for the rest of the tour.*

The funeral began in front of the Spies House at 10:00 in the morning; Spies' coffin was placed on a wagon and the family rode in a carriage behind. By the time the funeral procession had reached the Engel House about 25,000 people were marching in the procession. Close to a half million people watched the procession along Milwaukee Avenue and along Wells Street in downtown Chicago.

64. HOLY TRINITY ORTHODOX CHURCH (1121 N. Leavitt)

Since there were no one-way streets at the time of the Haymarket Martyrs' Funeral we cannot follow the exact route back to Milwaukee Avenue. We will stop to look at a few interesting buildings and homes along our detoured route.

At the corner of Potomac and Leavitt Streets if you look in the distance to your left you will see the dome of Holy Trinity Orthodox Church. The building was designed by Louis Sullivan. The structure is painted yellow and white with a green roof. The building looks very Russian, but it still displays the unique decoration and design of other Sullivan buildings.

R.T. Crane brought to America many Russian and Ukranian workers whom he used as strikebreakers at his factory on Desplaines Street in front of which the Haymarket meeting took place. This is the same R.T. Crane that headed the "Committee of Twenty-five" that erected the Police Statue. These Russian and Ukranian workers had no place to worship, and so Crane agreed to help finance the construction of this church. Czar Nicholas II of Russia also gave $5,000 from his personal funds so that his former subjects in America would have a place to worship.

Although this church is not directly on our route you may wish to see it closer. Also of interest is the modern new addition to St. Mary of Nazareth Hospital across the street from the church, and the beautiful new Roberto Clemente High School a block away at Division and Western which was built for the expanding Puerto Rican community.

65. BELL STREET COTTAGES

Continue on Potomac Street and turn right onto Bell for two

blocks. On your left you will see typical workers' cottages, similar to those in the Pullman community. These buildings were built in the 1880's about the same time as George Pullman ordered the building of Pullman City.

Continue along Bell, past the Sabin School and turn right onto W. LeMoyne Street and go one block to Leavitt. Turn right at Leavitt and left when you reach Schiller, then procede eastward until you reach Hoyne and "Beer Row".

66. "BEER ROW" MANSIONS (1300, 1400, and 1500 Blocks of Hoyne)

The Goldblatts' House (1407 Hoyne) at the northeast corner of Schiller and Hoyne is a fascinating house and typical of many of the houses along "Beer Row". You may wish to get out of your car and walk both north and south a block or two and look at the interesting modest homes as well as great mansions that line this street.

This house is known in the neighborhood as the Goldblatts' house, but this is a myth: they never lived here. The legend probably got started because the Goldblatts' family had their first department store in this area. Both Goldblatts and Wieboldts got started on Milwaukee Avenue when this business area was filled at the turn-of-the-century with newly arrived immigrants. Both department stores thrived here and later moved to State Street.

The so-called Goldblatts' House was probably built in the 1870's. It is in the "Second Empire Style" a French style of architecture that was popular in America after the Civil War. This house probably had no architect, but was designed by looking at standardized plans and catalogues of materials. Since the owner wanted to impress the viewer, he set the house on plenty of land; then built a standard type Chicago townhouse of the period, placing an elaborate roof on top of the whole thing. The owner then selected from catalogues of materials expensive iron work for fences, balconies, and entrance ways.

Additional iron work once lined the top of the roof, but it has been removed. The design of the carriage house at the rear is more pleasing in proportion and design.

If you walk north along the east side of Hoyne you will see several interesting houses.

The Johnson House at 1417 Hoyne was built in the 1870's, and it is well cared for. There is a beautiful gazebo at the south side of the house and a carriage house at the back.

The House at 1421 Hoyne was built in the 1870's when Mr. Wicker first developed the area, but the house was remodeled in the 1880's and the style was changed.

The House at 1427 Hoyne dates from the late 1880's, and it is built in the "Romanesque Style". Note particularly the leaded stained glass windows that illuminate the main staircase on the northside of the building.

The Waixel-Borgmeir House at 1521 Hoyne was originally built in the 1870's. The original title shows that it was built by Isaac Waixel, who sold over $20 million worth of meat to the federal government during the Civil War. Waixel was a "Cattle Baron" from New York, who moved to Chicago when the meat industry became centered here. This house once had a huge gazebo as well as a carriage house, but the latter burned down in recent years.

The name of Adolph Borgmeir is also associated with the house. Borgmeir was a master chairmaker with the A.P. Johnson Company, and it was probably Borgmeir that did the beautiful wood work on both the inside and outside of the house.

This home is now owned by Jeff Baily, a real estate sales consultant, who is promoting the restoration of this section of Wicker Park.

The Schlitz House once stood at the southeast corner of Hoyne and Pierce and it was because of Joseph Schlitz and other beer manufacturers who lived here that this street became known as "Beer Row". The huge estate of Joseph Schlitz was torn down in the 1920's to make way for several apartment buildings.

67. FORMER HOME OF NELSON ALGREN (1958 Evergreen)

SERBIAN CLUB RESTAURANT (1926 Evergreen)

Continue east on Schiller and turn right onto Damen and then left into Evergreen Street, which will take us to Milwaukee Avenue and the route of the Haymarket Martyr's funeral. But first there are a few spots of interest on curving, narrow Evergreen Street.

Nelson Algren, Chicago author, lived for many years at 1958 Evergreen. He was the author of the prose poem "Chicago, City on the Make" in which he described Wicker Park in this way:

". . . *old men play cards in the park" a neighborhood smelling of "Polish pierogis and Serbian shish-kabob."*

Algren was best known for his story "The Man with the Golden Arm" which was made into a movie. Wicker Park was the setting of this film. In March of 1975 Algren was quoted as saying "There just are not any neighborhoods here any more", and he announced he was moving out of the city.

Many Serbians moved into Wicker Park before and after World War I, and the Serbian Club Restaurant for many years served this ethnic community. The restaurant was sold in 1974 to new owners but until mid-1974 this restaurant was highly recommended by the *Chicago Guide* for food like Raznjici (a kind of shish-kabab), cevapcici (fresh grilled sausage), as well as things like sarma and moussaka. The music inside was also Serbian, and you could get all kinds of wines plus slivoivice.

68. FORMER SERBIAN CHURCH (Southwest corner of Evergreen and Schiller)

This rather unique little church in cream colored brick was for many years the church of the Serbian community, but it was sold about 1973.

The church was purchased by a Puerto Rican congregation that has renovated the building. Today Wicker Park is about half Puerto Rican.

69. SERBIAN BROTHERS HELP, INC. (1911 Evergreen)

This Serbian organization still operates in the community helping fellow Serbians with their problems. Historically all ethnic groups formed organizations to protect the new arrivals who were being exploited by their employers, and discriminated against by the established residents of the city.

There are still a number of other Serbian organizations in Wicker Park and the surrounding area. They include the Serbian National Defense Council, the Serbian Literary Association, the Serbian Singing Federation, the Serbian Weekly Sloboda, and a Serbian radio program.

Just as August Spies had tried to establish a German language worker newspaper to provide communication within his ethnic group, there are still many ethnic newspapers, clubs, and schools existing among the approximately 80 different ethnic groups in the Chicago Metropolitan Area today.

70. MILWAUKEE AVENUE AND THE HAYMARKET MARTYRS' FUNERAL PROCESSION

At Evergreen and Milwaukee Avenue turn right. We are now following the route of the Martyrs' Funeral.

Many of the old business buildings along this street have the names of the builders and the date of construction on the cornices at the tops of the buildings. Many of the dates are 1887 and earlier, and you can be sure that people were leaning out of the windows of these buildings to catch a glimpse of the funeral procession as it passed on Sunday, November 13, 1887.

Milwaukee Avenue was once known as "Dinner Pail Avenue", since this was the heart of the working class neighborhood in the 1880's. This was the ideal route for the funeral procession. The authorities however were apprehensive. The Daily News reported the following:

"Special conditions were laid down by Mayor Roche of Chicago under which the public funeral was to be conducted. The line of

Milwaukee Avenue "Dinner Pail Avenue", scene of the Haymarket Martyrs' Funeral (Courtesy Chicago Historical Society)

march was precisely delineated; no banner, flags, or arms were to be displayed; no music except dirges was to be played; no demonstration was to be made; no speeches were to be delivered; it was to be held (through the downtown area) between twelve and two o'clock. From beginning to end the funeral procession was subject to police regulation and surveillance."

Milwaukee Avenue has changed very little over the years. One author described conditions on this street in the 1880's in this way:

"The workday began in the dark hours of the early morning, as early as 4 a.m. for those with over two or three miles to walk (since they could not afford Yerkes' streetcars that cost 10¢ which was two hours wages for the women and children). By six o'clock thousands of men, women, and children were trudging down streets like Milwaukee Avenue. . . Dinner buckets in hand, not to return until early evening. In 1882 bakers were found working 15 to 17 hours a day around hot ovens, with little time for food or rest. Brewery employees labored from 3 a.m. to 6 p.m. in the busy season. Sailors on the Great Lakes worked 15 hour stints for days on end. Street car drivers and conductors worked 15 and 16 hours, often split into early morning and evening shifts."

It was in the struggle for the "Eight Hour Day" that the Haymarket Martyrs' had died, and the people along Milwaukee Avenue who worked long hours turned out to show their respect to these men.

In 1951, Nelson Algren wrote the following about Milwaukee Avenue:

"Cruising down Milwaukee Avenue on any Loop-bound trolley on any weekday morning, the straphangers to Success who keep the factories and the ginmills running stand reading the papers that could as well be published in Israel or Athens, in Warsaw or in Rome. On either side of the cartracks are the shops with the American signs in one window and . . . in the other: Spanish, Polish, Italian, Hebrew, Chinese or Greek."

As you drive up Milwaukee Avenue notice how many of these foreign signs and ethnic workers are still here today.

71. HOME OF THE FISCHER FAMILY (1336 Dean Street, near the corner of Milwaukee and Paulina)

When the funeral procession reached Paulina Street it turned left and then left again to Dean Street, which runs parallel to

The Fischer home

Milwaukee. Here the funeral procession stopped to pick up the second body, that of Adolph Fischer.

The shell of the Fischer House was still standing in 1975, after it had been gutted by fire in 1974. Before the fire, the house looked exactly as it had in 1887 when Fischer's coffin was placed on a wagon and his wife and three children joined the funeral cortege.

The Daily News described the scene on November 13, 1887:

"They soon arrived at the desolate and poverty-stricken home of Mrs. Fischer, where the hearse containing Adolph Fischer's body joined the procession."

Adolph Fischer, who was a compositer for the Arbeiter-Zeitung, had very little to do with the Haymarket meeting. Fischer attended the so-called "Monday Night Conspiracy Meeting" at Grief's Hall (See No. 6) on the evening of May 3, 1886, to plan the Haymarket Meeting. It was Fischer who inserted the line "Workingmen Arm Yourselves and Appear In Full Force" on about 200 copies of the flyers announcing the meeting. August Spies was furious when he saw these words, and he said he would not speak at the rally unless the line were removed. Fischer then threw the 200 copies with this line into the waste basket, and printed 20,000 without the line, which were distributed throughout the city.

Fischer did attend the Haymarket Meeting, but left for Zepf's Hall when Parsons finished speaking about ten o'clock. He was among those who threw themselves on the floor of Zepf's Hall to avoid the bullets that came through the windows. He never really knew what had happened on Desplaines street until the next morning when he read the paper while riding the streetcar up Milwaukee Avenue to downtown Chicago and the offices of the Arbeiter-Zeitung.

At 10:30 a.m. Captain Bonfield raided the offices of the Arbeiter-Zeitung, and Fischer was arrested. Copies of the original "Workingmen Arm Yourselves. . ." flyer were found in the waste basket and used as evidence against Fischer. He was then taken to the jail at Central Police Headquarters in the City Hall Building.

Fischer was born in Bremen, Germany in about 1860. He attended school for 8 ½ years, which meant he was very well educated for those times.

He sailed for the United States when he was 15 and went to work for his older brother William B. Fischer who had come to Little Rock, Arkansas a number of years before. Adolph Fischer became an apprentice compositer on his brother's German language paper.

Fischer joined the German Typographical Union in St. Louis, Missouri in 1879, and was married in that city in 1881. He arrived in Chicago with his family on June 1, 1883 and went to work for the Arbeiter-Zeitung and its editor August Spies.

Fischer had read the writings of Thomas Paine and Thomas Jefferson and greatly admired both of them. He felt that the worker of the 1880's was being duped. He was concerned with the new machines that were eliminating jobs as well as the poor distribution of wealth.

Fischer was only 27 years old when he was hung. He had three children, a girl, and two boys that were all very young at the time. The Pioneer Aid and Support Society received money from all over the world to help support the family after Fischer's death. His wife eventually remarried.

Fischer's funeral was planned and paid for by his union brothers in Typographical Union No. 9.

Milwaukee, Division, and Ashland Business District and Schoenhofen Hall (Courtesy Chicago Historical Society)

72. MILWAUKEE, DIVISION, ASHLAND BUSINESS DISTRICT

Although Milwaukee Avenue around North Avenue was a German neighborhood in 1886, the area around Milwaukee, Division, and Ashland was at that time a Polish neighborhood and it is still partly Polish today. Division street was known as "Polish Broadway", but today Division Street is the heart of the Puerto Rican community.

The site of the Walgreen's store at the northwest corner of Milwaukee and Ashland was once the site of Schoehofen Hall which was built in 1884 and used for many union meetings.

At the northeast corner of Milwaukee Avenue and Division Street you'll see a white terracotta building which once housed the offices of the Polish Daily Zgoda. In 1920, there were five daily Polish papers in Chicago. Today, only two weekly Polish papers are published.

The Polish workers of this community helped raise money during World War I to send troops to Europe to help free Poland from Russia. During World War II, they raised money to pay for a bomber which was named "Chicago Polonia", and it was flown by a young man from the community named Roman Pucinski, who would later be a U.S. Congressman and Alderman of the City of Chicago.

Pucinski once said that it was necessary for the Polish workers to band together and set up newspapers and later radio stations because the city was ". . . not friendly to Slavic people . . . ."

Today the Polish community of Chicago still supports orphanages in Poland, as well as disabled Polish veterans of World War II in England.

If you wish to get a little of the feeling of the Polish community stop by the **F and T Sandwich Shop** at 1182 Milwaukee Avenue just south of the intersection. It certainly doesn't look like much from the outside, and the inside looks like something out of the 1930's, but the Polish food they serve is wonderful!

The Parsons home at the time of the funeral

73. FORMER HOME OF LUCY PARSONS (Formerly at 1129 Milwaukee Avenue)
HOLY TRINITY CHURCH
NOBLE SQUARE COOPERATIVE HOUSING PROJECT

Although the original building at 1129 Milwaukee that was occupied by Lucy Parsons and her two children in 1887 has been demolished, if you look across the street to 1124 Milwaukee Avenue you will see a building that is identical in appearance to the former Parsons' home.

Lucy could no longer afford the apartment at 1120 W. Grand Avenue where they were living at the time of the Haymarket Meeting, and she moved to this 3rd floor walk-up apartment at the time of the Haymarket Trial.

Albert Parsons' body was returned to this spot shortly before 11:00 a.m. on the morning of Saturday, November 12, 1887. The Daily News described the arrival of the body:

"When the street door was opened, Mrs. Parsons was observed at the head of the stairs dressed in a long black wrapper. Apparently she had rested little during last night for her eyes were swollen with much weeping. She was greatly excited when she realized that they were about to bring up her dead husband, and she immediately commenced weeping again. A committee went to her and endeavored to calm her, but she grew more agitated until they almost forced her into her apartment and locked the door. She would not listen to their entreaties, and one was left to see that she did herself no harm, while the others carried up the coffin and deposited it on two chairs in the little sitting room. The top of the casket was removed and the calm, pale features exposed.

All the time they were taking off the lid, Mrs. Parsons was struggling in the room adjoining and calling the name of her husband. Little Albert and Lulu, the fatherless children, stood together, crying and unnoticed in the corner of the room. When the chamber door was unlocked, the widow rushed out and threw herself bodily on the coffin. An hysterical cry escaped her lips, and the poor woman fell on the floor in a dead faint before her friends could catch her."

On Sunday, November 13, this was the third stop for the funeral procession. Albert's body was placed on a wagon, and Lucy and the children joined the funeral cortege.

The Noble Square Cooperative Housing Project occupies the former site of Parsons' home. The red brick building with the number 1127 is closest to the exact site. It is fitting that a low income housing project of this type should occupy this site.

Noble Square is far better planned than the average housing project. It includes $17,000 townhouses and cooperative appartments in the 28 story high rise at Milwaukee and Division. This complex was planned with the cooperation of Polish groups and community organizations in the neighborhood in order to avoid the bad planning in other projects such as Cabrini Green and the Robert Taylor Homes.

Holy Trinity Church and School can been seen directly behind the former site of the Parsons' home. The first interest of this parish after its founding in 1873 was in school construction since bilingual education was crucial to the preservation and improvement of the Polish community. The early pastor who carried out this work was Father Casimer Sztuczko. The original elementary school buildings were designed by John Wierzbieniec, but later replaced by the dark red brick structures you now see, which were designed by the Rogers Co. in 1916 at a cost of $280,000.

The strikingly beautiful Holy Trinity Church with its twin green copper spires was built much later to replace the original old frame church. The first architectural sketches of the church were made by the Polish architect, Olszewski, who lived in Washington D.C. at the time. Olszewski designed such a grand church that the parish turned it down because it would be too costly, and the State of Illinois refused to allow Olszewski, as a licensed Polish architect, to practice in this state. Eventually another architect, William Krieg, took the designs, modified them, and construction began on April 2, 1905. The church was completed on Oct. 6, 1906 and dedicated by Archbishop Quigley.

Holy Trinity Church is of "Romanesque Style" with twin towers and a beautiful Grecian facade. When the area between the church and the Kennedy Expressway was cleared for the Noble Square Project, a mall was set aside in front of the church and from here one can get an impressive view of the church. The church building is of pressed brick and limestone, and iron was used in the construction of the structure.

In 1910, a high school was started by this very active parish, and it grew rapidly. Eventually the parish purchased the old Koscuisko Public High School on Division Street from the Board of Education, and it was remodeled to serve the needs of the Polish young people.

While most classes were taught in English in the early days, religion, Polish history, and literature were taught in Polish.

The building of yellowish pressed brick to the south of the church was built in 1914 as a new Rectory. It was designed by the Rogers Co. at a cost of $41,000.

This parish has always been very active in producing plays and musical productions. Lydia Pucinski, the mother of the former Congressman, has worked on these theatrical productions for over forty years.

74. FORMER SITE OF TIMMERHOF HALL (1049 Milwaukee)
FUR AND LEATHER WORKERS HALL (1405 Cortez, near the intersection of Milwaukee and Noble.

Timmerhof Hall was mentioned in Captain Schaack's book "Anarchy and the Anarchists" as a meeting place for the union anarchists who Schaack said wished to destroy Chicago and kill its businessmen. Timmerhof Hall was a frame building, and an old brick structure now occupies the site.

Just around the corner from the former site of Timmerhof Hall at the intersection of Milwaukee, Noble and Cortez is a building owned by the Fur and Leather Workers Union. This hall at 1405 Cortez was formerly known as Walsh's Hall, and President McKinley is supposed to have once spoken here. The Fur and Leather Workers purchased the building in 1948 for their Joint Board Headquarters.

Timmerhof Hall

Although the fur and leather industry is not as large in Chicago as it once was, there was a time when hides from the Stock Yards were carried down the Chicago River to Goose Island and ethnic workers from this community worked long hours under unsafe conditions in the tanneries.

In 1954, the Fur and Leather Workers merged with the Amalgamated Meat Cutters.

75. THE POLISH MUSEUM OF AMERICA AND THE POLISH ROMAN CATHOLIC UNION (984 Milwaukee)

One block further up Milwaukee Avenue on the southwest corner of Milwaukee and Augusta Avenue is the building of the Polish Roman Catholic Union which also houses the Polish Museum of America.

The Polish Roman Catholic Union was established over 100 years ago in 1873. One of the founders was Father Vincent

Barzynski (See No. 54) who saw this as an extension of the work of his church, St. Stanislaus.

The Polish Roman Catholic Union is a fraternal insurance company. Besides the payment of death benefits to the beneficiaries of its members, the union gives aid to its crippled members. It also has an educational fund from which indigent students receive aid.

The museum was organized in 1935 by the President of the Polish Roman Catholic Union at that time, Joseph L. Kania. The name Polish Museum of America was adopted in 1961, and the museum "is a repository of the culture of the Polish people, the men and women of America of Polish descent who have played an important part in the building of America."

Efforts are now being made to make the museum a depository of information about early Polish immigration and the problems of Polish workers in America. A great deal of translation must be done since all these early letters and newspaper stories are in Polish.

Included in the museum collection are many things associated with the pianist and statesman, Paderewski, the General Kosciuszko collection, and the Polish exhibit from the New York World's Fair of 1939. The museum is open Monday through Saturday from 10 a.m. to 4 p.m.

76. FORMER SITES OF THALIA HALL AND THE HOME OF GOTTFRIED WALLER (Now the site of the Kennedy Expressway and the Milwaukee Avenue Overpass)

All of the old community in this area has been leveled to make way for the Kennedy Expressway, which is jokingly referred to as "The Polish Corridor" by the Poles of this community since it cut their community in half in the same way the "Polish Corridor" at Danzig cut Germany off from East Prussia after World War I.

Thalia Hall was once located at 968 Milwaukee Avenue, and this hall served Chicago Cooperative Association Union Beer that was sold to the workers at lower prices than Schlitz and the beer of the other "Beer Barons" of Wicker Park. During the Haymarket Trial Captain Schaack had members of his "Red Squad" in this hall listening to what the workers were saying about the Haymarket Trial and getting lists of names of possible future troublemakers.

Near Thalia Hall was the home of Gottfried Waller, who originally proposed the Haymarket Meeting at Grief's Hall on May 3, 1886. Waller turned State's witness and testified against his friend George Engel. Engel was executed and Waller went free. Could Gottfried Waller have been in the pay of Inspector Bonfield and Captain Schaack in order to set up meetings and demonstrations and create possible confrontations? By 1889, it was uncovered that the police were involved in this type of infiltration of unions and community groups. Maybe this is why Waller was never brought to trial? We'll never know!

77. INTERSECTION OF MILWAUKEE, CHICAGO, AND OGDEN AVENUES AND ST. JOHN CANTIUS CHURCH

This intersection was once one of the busiest in the City of Chicago. Today it is very quiet and almost deserted. Baer's Hall, an early meeting hall, still stands at the southwest corner of the intersection.

To the left as you approach the intersection you will see St.

John Cantius Church and School. Because St. Stanislaus Church could only hold 5,000 people for the Sunday morning services, and Holy Trinity was also overcrowded, it was necessary in the 1890's to found another parish near this once busy intersection. These three churches are quite close together and they were always full. Imagine how densely populated this area once was with Polish workers.

Rev. Father Barzynski appointed Father John Kasprzycki to form this new parish, and a large plot of land at Chicago Avenue, Carpenter, and Fry Streets was purchased in 1893 for $75,000. In the same year construction began on the church which took five years to complete. The architect of the church was Mr. A. Druiding, and the cost of construction in 1898 when it was completed was $130,000.

The church is in the "Roman Style"; the walls are of a dark pressed brick, and the front of the church is of cut stone. It is 107 feet wide and 230 long, and once held as many as 2,000 Polish Catholics each Sunday.

The once busy intersection of Milwaukee, Chicago, and Ogden Avenues with Baer's Hall on the right. (Courtesy Chicago Historical Society)

The right tower of the church is most impressive with its clock and green copper roof.

The parochial school building still stands along Chicago Avenue. It was erected in 1905 and by 1920 over 2,000 children were attending this school. Today the school is almost empty and the descendants of these children have moved northwest along Milwaukee Avenue to the edge of the city and the suburbs.

78. FORMER SITE OF AURORA TURNER HALL
(Milwaukee and Huron)

A Clark Service Station at Huron Street now occupies the site of the Aurora Turner Hall. It was from this hall that workers marched on April 21, 1855 at the time of the so-called "Lager Beer Riots" when Mayor Boone tried to shut down the saloons and German beer gardens.

These Turner Halls and other such halls were necessary when the ethnic workers lived crowded into one or two rooms. They could come here to talk with friends, have meetings, dances and weddings.

Several of the Haymarket Martyrs were members of the

Aurora Turners, and this hall was used for a memorial service on Saturday, November 12. The hall was draped in black as the funeral procession passed on Sunday.

A short distance down the street is a very old building at 686 Milwaukee (now the Victory Store). Captain Schaack and his men raided this building shortly after the Haymarket bombing. Schaack claimed he had reports that bombs were being stored here. None were found.

Across the street from 686 Milwaukee are a number of old buildings that were still standing in 1975, but will probably be demolished soon. These buildings are typical of the kind that once lined Milwaukee Avenue all the way into downtown Chicago.

79. FORMER SITE OF ENGEL TOY STORE AND HOME
(630 Milwaukee)

The Engel toy store and home is gone, but it stood near the southwest corner of Erie and Milwaukee, where today there is a greenbelt next to the Ohio Street cut-off of the Kennedy Expressway.

Sunday, November 13, the funeral procession stopped here to pick up the last two bodies; those of George Engel and Louis Lingg.

The Engel toy store and home (2nd floor)

Lingg's body was brought here because he had no family in America. Lingg's teenage sweetheart, Ida Mueller, and Mary Engel, the teenage daughter of George, had become good friends during the trial, the appeal, and the terrible period before the execution. The Engel family took charge of the body of Lingg after the supposed suicide, and the International Carpenters Union paid for all his funeral expenses, since he was a union brother.

George Engel, who lived here with his wife and children never even attended the Haymarket Meeting. He was playing cards with friends and drinking beer in their second floor apartment when Waller rushed in and told him what had happened. It was nearly a week before he was finally arrested in his home. His only connection with Haymarket was the fact that he attended two meetings. One near Clybourn Avenue on May 2, 1886 of the Northwestside Group of the International Workingmen's Party of America when the workers discussed what they would do if Pinkerton detectives or police tried to attack the strikers during their marches that week for the "Eight Hour Day". The other meeting he attended was the one in the basement of Grief's Hall after the workers had been shot and killed at the McCormick Reaper Plant on May 3. This is the meeting at which Gottfried Waller proposed the rally to be held in Haymarket Square on May 4.

Engel was the oldest of the Haymarket Eight at 51 years of age. He was born in Cassel, Germany on April 15, 1836, the son of a mason and bricklayer who died when he was only 18 months old. When he was 12 years old his mother also died.

The government gave him $15 a month until he was fourteen years old, and then he was expected to learn a trade, so he became an apprentice painter. He worked as a painter for many years, but in 1863 at the age of twenty-seven he became interested in social questions while living in Bremen.

In 1866 he moved to the City of Leipzig, married two years later, and set up his own small business. But industrialization in Germany was destroying many small businessmen and Engel was one of them. In 1866, at the age of thirty, he immigrated to America. He worked in Philadelphia in 1873 as a painter and later a worker in a sugar refinery.

Things seemed to be getting better when suddenly he became ill. Medicine and doctors took all his money, his wife and children were starving, and he was forced to turn to the Philadelphia German Aid Society for help. It took him over a year to recover.

In 1874, he came to Chicago and worked at the Tembruth Wagon Factory, and became active in the labor movement. He was impressed in Chicago by the humanity and sacrifice made for the good of others by members of the workingmen's societies.

In 1876, after his health improved, he opened this store on Milwaukee Avenue. The store provided him with time and independence, and he became more involved in labor questions.

He became very discouraged with the democratic election process after Judge Gardner of Chicago refused to punish ballot-box stuffers, causing Parsons and the Socialist-Labor Party to lose in several close elections.

Engel was especially devoted to his teenage daughter, Mary, who tried to cheer him up while he was in jail. She spent as much time with him as possible toward the end.

On Saturday, November 12, the bodies of Engel and Lingg were placed on public display in the back room of the toy store. The Daily News reported the following:

"The door of the little cigar and toy store, which Mrs. Engel had managed since the arrest of her husband, was draped in mourning. A red-faced man with a white mustache stood on a box in the center of the door and separated those going in from those going out.

In the back room lay the bodies of Louis Lingg, the suicide, and Engel. They were in their coffins, and no one was permitted to take more than one look as he passed along . . .

Hardly one out of twenty who go into the Engel store to view the remains speak their minds in English . . . the babble on the sidewalk and in the gutter . . . was sometimes loud enough to be heard far down the avenue. The people came from all directions. . . . men, women, children and girls. Every car, both from across the bridge and from the extremes of Milwaukee Avenue, deposited several people who rushed and pushed and often swore to get a place in the line . . . Now and then a detective from the central station loomed up, but he came and went so as not to attract attention. . . . If the men knew that "Bonfield's Spies" heard every excited threat they are uttering over the dead bodies of their heroes there might be trouble. Often a very excited man would raise his hand and utter fearful oaths in German. Often the name of Bonfield could be distinguished in their rantings.

It is estimated that ten thousand people passed in to see Lingg and Engel today."

80. THE COMO INN (546 Milwaukee Avenue) AND THE INTERSECTION OF MILWAUKEE, GRAND AND HALSTED

Continuing along Milwaukee Avenue you pass over the Ohio Street cut-off of the Kennedy Expressway, and you'll see that this entire area that once housed thousands of ethnic workers has been wiped out.

Although this area had been German and Polish in the 1880's, eventually many Italians moved from the area east of here, known as "Little Sicily", around the Montgomery Ward warehouses that you see in the distance across the river on your left. By the 1920's this was entirely an Italian neighborhood.

The Como Inn which has been owned by the same Italian family since 1924 is the only thing Italian left. It is highly recommended by Chicago Magazine and it specializes in chicken cacciatore, roast or baked pheasant, and seafood such as calamari, abalone, pompano, and lobster.

"Little Sicily" or "Little Hell" was the name given to the ethnic neighborhood across the river to the east of the Como Inn. Harvey Zorbaugh described this area in a book he wrote in 1929:

"Into this slum district along the river, and in the vicinity of this industrial area, which had been first Irish and then Swedish, had been known as Kilgubbin, as Little Hell, and lastly as Smokey Hollow, began to come in the late nineties, the Italian — the Italian from the southern island of Sicily. He came in small numbers at first. But with the opening years of the twentieth century came a Sicilian wave, part of the great Italian immigration of 1903-4, and the Sicilian began to take possession of the Irish and Swedish community between Sedgwick Street and the industrial belt along the river. This wave reached its crest about 1906.

While the Irish and Swedish had gotten on well as neighbors, neither could or would live peaceably with the Sicilian. There was considerable friction, especially among the children . . . alley garbage cans were stripped of their covers which served as shields in these encounters."

In the 1930's under Roosevelt's New Deal, new housing was built for the Italians, the Mother Cabrini Housing Project, named for the saint who once worked in this area. By the 1950's the area had become black and more of the area was leveled for the huge prison-like high rises you see in the distance that are known as Cabrini-Green. The Green is for William Green, former President of the American Federation of Labor. For nearly 140 years this area has been a dumping ground for immigrant and migrant workers coming to Chicago that no one wanted in their neighborhood. It has always been a troubled area.

Continue a short distance along Milwaukee and you are at the once busy intersection of Milwaukee, Grand and Halsted.

Although not on the tour route, there are three former home sites of the Parsons family on Grand Avenue that are located three to seven blocks west of the intersection.

The Parsons' home in 1884 at 1511 Grand Avenue, which is a small well kept house. They were living here at the time that Albert and Lucy led the Thanksgiving Day "Poor People's Marches" past the mansions on Rush Street and Prairie Avenue.

The Parsons' home in 1885 at 1374 Grand Avenue was an apartment over a store. Albert and Lucy opened a dress shop and tailor shop in the store, since they needed to supplement their income. Albert only received a small salary as editor of the Alarm, and he had been blacklisted since 1877 by the business community.

The Parsons' home in 1886 at 1120 Grand Avenue was also an apartment over a store. A small grocery store now occupies the ground floor. It was from this apartment that Albert, Lucy, Lizzie Holmes and the children walked that night to the corner of Halsted and Randolph to catch a streetcar into the Loop (See No. 12). After Albert was indicted, the police watched this apartment day and night and constantly trailed Lucy when she left it, hoping to follow her to find Albert. After Albert turned himself in to stand trial she could not afford the rent here and moved to the apartment on Milwaukee Avenue (See No. 73).

81. DESPLAINES STREET VIADUCT (Desplaines Street south of Kinzie)

Continue along Milwaukee Avenue, through the underpass, and then angle slightly to the right on to the Desplaines Street Viaduct.

The police had not wished the funeral procession to go into the heart of the downtown area, so this route was selected.

Immediately after leaving Zepf's Hall, on May 4, Lucy, Albert, Lizzie Holmes and the children came here after the shooting had stopped (See No. 5). Lizzie Holmes later wrote about the conversation that took place here.

"Mr. and Mrs. Parsons and myself started up the Desplaines street viaduct to go home, and shortly afterward Thomas Brown joined us. I said to Mr. Parsons:

'I do not know what has happened, or whether there is any further danger, but we may be sure some kind of a conflict has occurred. Everybody knows you and they all know your influence. If any of our boys are in danger you are. Whatever has happened, leave the city for a few days at least. We can't spare you yet, and in the excited condition the people must be in we do not know what might happen to you.'

Then Parsons said:

'I do not think I ought to go—do you?'

Lizzie Holmes replies:

'Yes—go; there is no harm in going away for a few days until we see what is the matter and have time to collect our thoughts and

determine what is best to do; you do not want to be taken unawares; be at a safe distance, and when you see you are needed come, as I know you always will."

"Many other arguments I used to induce the brave, home-loving man to depart before he at last consented. He had not money enough with him to go far and Mr. Brown quickly tendered him $5. It was decided best for his wife not to accompany him, so there on the viaduct we separated, Brown going one way, Mrs. Parsons another, and we two toward the Northwestern depot (which was then located at the present site of the Merchandise Mart facing Wells Street)."

Just before he turned away Parsons said:

'Kiss me, Lucy. We do not know when we will meet again'. . . and there seemed a sad, almost prophetic, tone in his voice. . . "

Parsons took the train that night to Turner Junction (now West Chicago), since he could not reach the Holmes house in Geneva, Illinois by train until the next morning. He stayed with Mr. Holmes for several days, while Lizzie Holmes continued to stay in Chicago with Lucy and the children. Parsons and Mr. Holmes then decided that Geneva wasn't safe and on May 10, Parsons went to stay with Daniel Hoan of Waukesha, Wisconsin where he grew a beard, dressed in old clothes, and worked as a carpenter for over one month.

Another event happened on the railroad tracks below this viaduct after Parsons left Waukesha on the evening of Sunday, June 20 in order to arrive in Chicago early on the morning of June 21 to turn himself in at the opening session of the trial. Parsons wished to be tried with his friends, although there is no question he was safe and probably could have avoided the death penalty. Lucy Parsons described what happened that morning:

"As the train neared Kinzie street, slowing up as usual at this point, Mr. Parsons thought best to alight there, rather than to go to the depot. Morning was mistily dawning, and the great city lay in shrouded silence. He leaped from the train, which was gliding along at a swifter rate than he had calculated upon, and fell, rolling over once or twice before he caught himself. A policeman who stood near came and assisted him to his feet."

'Are yez hurt, now?' queried the servant of the law, feeling over him for broken bones.

'No, I thank ye, (Parsons) answered awkwardly . . . 'only shaken up a bit . . . I be all right in a minit or two.'

"The policeman allowed the little old farmer to walk away, never dreaming that he had put his hands on the much-wanted Parsons . . . "

82. FULTON STREET MARKET (West along Fulton at Desplaines)

Continuing across the over-pass on Desplaines you will see on your right at Fulton another of Chicago's markets, which is only a short distance from the Haymarket. The Fulton Market was once the fish market for the city.

83. LAKE STREET UNION HALLS AND THE LAKE STREET BRIDGE (Along Lake from Desplaines to Wacker Drive)

When the funeral procession for the Haymarket Martyrs

Florus' Hall with its co-operative saloon, restaurant, and meeting rooms.

reached Lake Street it turned left at Zepf's Hall and continued east along Lake into the downtown area.

The procession was now within half a block of the site of the Haymarket meeting that had taken place a year and a half before. Zepf's Hall was draped in black as were all the German beer gardens and union halls along the entire route from Wicker Park.

Just two blocks east of Zepf's Hall was Florus' Hall and assembly rooms where many unions held their meetings. This hall was owned by Albert Florus, who ran a restaurant for workers in the area and a co-operative saloon. Florus was considered a "red" by Schaack and the police, and for years after the funeral his place was under surveillance and those who went in were subject to investigation.

Grief's Hall was also draped in black as the funeral passed. It was here that Gottfired Waller had first suggested the meeting that led to the tragedy.

Both Grief's Hall and Florus' Hall were raided again by the police in 1891. After the scandals connected with the discharge of Bonfield and Schaack the businessmen decided to stop making payoffs to the police. They had been giving the police from $50,000 to $140,000 annually to find "reds." By 1891, members of the Union League Club and the Commercial Club felt all the "subversives" had surely been weeded out. But suddenly, upon hearing about the end of the payoffs, the police began to raid unions halls and announce the discovery of new bomb plots all over the city.

The funeral procession now crossed over the Chicago River on the Lake Street bridge. In order to get a better view of the coffins and the families of the Martyrs as well as the rest of the 25,000 people in the procession, people climbed all over the steel structure of this bridge.

84. FORMER SITE OF THE WIGWAM AND LINCOLN'S NOMINATION IN 1860 (Southeast corner of Lake and Wacker Drive)

After crossing the Chicago River, the funeral procession passed the former site of the "Wigwam," a huge pineboard political hall that was built in April of 1860 to seat 5,000 people. Actually it had over 10,000 delegates packed into it when Lincoln was nominated here on May 18, 1860. A plaque once marked this corner, and its outline can still be seen on the building on the southeast corner. The plaque was stolen in 1974.

Two people who occupied this building in 1860 would affect the lives of the Haymarket Martyrs and their families.

The first would be Joseph Medill, later Mayor of Chicago and editor of the Tribune, who used his paper to demand the execution of Parsons and the others. In this hall Medill told the chairmen of the Ohio delegation, when Lincoln needed only 4 more votes . . . "If you can throw Ohio to Lincoln, you can have anything you want!" It was this statement that got Lincoln nominated.

The second person who affected the lives of the Haymarket Eight was Abraham Lincoln. Lucy Parsons and other American Black workers would be freed by the "Great Emancipator," and Lincoln's words on the rights of workers would inspire Parsons and the others to fight for shorter hours and democracy on the job.

If all Americans had listened to the words of Lincoln there would have been no Haymarket Affair. Lincoln said:

"Thank God we live in a country where the workingman has the right to strike."

"Capital is the fruit of labor and would never have existed if labor had not existed first."

"Workingmen are the basis of all government."

The Republican Party, the businessmen of Chicago, and the police had forgotten the principles of Lincoln by 1886.

85. THE OFFICES OF ATTORNEY JOSEPH M. JACOBS AND THE ROOSEVELT COLLECTION (201 N. Wells, 19th Floor)
OFFICES OF THE CHICAGO FEDERATION OF TEACHERS (201 N. Wells, 9th Floor)

The funeral procession turned right at the corner of Lake and Wells Streets. On the northeast corner of Lake and Wells in the 201 N. Wells Building are the offices of Joseph M. Jacobs, Chairman of the Executive Board of the Illinois Labor History Society. Mr. Jacobs, a distinguished labor attorney, has the most extensive collections of Roosevelt letters, campaign buttons, and mementoes outside the Roosevelt Collection in Hyde Park, New York. Some of the collection has been given to the University of Illinois at Chicago Circle, but a significant collection of artifacts and memorabilia remains on view here.

Many of the things that the Haymarket Eight sought in 1886 became law during the New Deal Administration of Franklin Delano Roosevelt.

Also located here are the offices of the Chicago Federation of Teachers, Local 1 of the American Federation of Teachers. An excellent history of Chicago teachers can be found in, "The Chicago Schools" by Mary J. Herrick, a member of this local (also see No. 33).

86. SITE OF THE STEUBEN CLUB (Now the 188 W. Randolph Building, northeast corner of Wells and Randolph)

Wells Street (which was then called Fifth Avenue) was selected for the march through the downtown area because it was the location of many German newspapers, clubs, and workers' organizations.

This great "Gothic Style" skyscraper was built in the 1920's to replace an earlier building used by the Steuben Club. The Steuben Club contained hotel rooms, a swimming pool, and athletic facilities for German businessmen who were discriminated against at the Union League Club or the Commercial Club. The club went bankrupt with the 1929 crash and the building was turned into commercial offices. This building presently houses the offices of the International Brotherhood of Electrical Workers, Local 336, as well as several other unions.

87. THE BISMARCK HOTEL (Southeast corner of Wells and Randolph)
FORMER SITE OF THE STAATS-ZEITUNG NEWSPAPER (Now a vacant lot, formerly at northeast corner of Wells and Washington)

Again testifying to the German character of this street in

The Staats-Zietung Building and on the right the building where the Chicago Federation of Labor was founded in 1896. (Courtesy Chicago Historical Society)

1886 and even today, you see the Bismarck Hotel which occupies nearly half the block between Randolph and Washington. In 1886, the German Consulate in Chicago was also on Wells.

At the next corner going south, the procession would have passed the office building of the oldest daily German paper west of New York, the Staats-Zeitung, which was owned by A.C. Hesing and later his son Washington Hesing. Although this paper was more conservative than the Arbeiter-Zeitung it supported the cause of the Haymarket Martyrs, and it supported the rights of other minority groups in Chicago.

After the Bread Riot of 1872, a People's Party was formed and in the election of December 1873 with the support of the Staats-Zeitung, Mayor Medill was defeated by the ethnic coalition candidate Mayor Colvin.

One German youth was so excited about this victory of the Germans over the Anglo-Saxons of the city, that he raised a Prussian flag from the flag pole on top the Staats-Zeitung Building. Medill of the Tribune published a horrified editorial on what was happening to America, when Germans were gaining control of its second largest city and raising foreign flags over Chicago.

The victory of the People's Party was very short. Within two years Medill and his friends had regained political control of the city and were determined never to lose it again.

Directly to the east of the Staats-Zeitung Building was a building famous as lodge-rooms and meeting places for all kinds of societies including the Knights of Labor. It was in this building in 1896 that the Chicago Federation of Labor was formed from Parson's old Trades and Labor Assembly.

88. FORMER SITE OF THE TIMES BUILDING (Now the Illinois Bell Telephone Building, northwest corner of Wells and Washington)

The five story Times Building stood here from 1872 until the 1920's when it was finally demolished. The structure was designed by Wilbur F. Storey specifically as a newspaper building. Besides the Times there were also offices of the Daily Freie Presse, another German language paper.

During the Haymarket Trial this paper was probably no more friendly to the Haymarket Eight than the Daily News or the Tribune, but shortly after the trial it was purchased by former Mayor Carter Harrison. Mayor Harrison had testified against the police in the Haymarket Trial and had lost reelection in 1887. Harrison wanted to become Mayor again, (he did in 1893), but he needed a newspaper to tell his side of the story. So he purchased the Times.

On January 4, 1889 James J. West, the editor of the Times, and Joseph R. Dunlop, the city editor, began a series of stories about Inspector Bonfield and Captain Schaack. Here are a few quotes:

"Bonfield proclaims to the world that the gamblers are gone and that the dens of vice are closed. But The Times knows of scores of places open to the public . . .

Bonfield still would shrug his shoulders, say 'there is no gambling in Chicago' and march off to look for some respectable German citizen whom he might arrest and call an anarchist."

"Police Engaged to Build, Repair, and Decorate Homes for Bonfield and Schaack"

Captain Schaack of the Chicago Avenue Police Station

As a result of stories like this West and Dunlop were served with an arrest warrant on January 5. They were not given time to assign the editorship to someone else and they were dragged to the police station and booked just as Parsons, Spies, and the others had been by Bonfield and Schaack three years before.

But this was too much since West and Dunlop were both members of the better clubs of the city. By January 15, Bonfield and Schaack were on there way out, but it was too late for justice for the Haymarket Martyrs.

This is what the Times wrote on January 15, 1889:

"The end of the official career of Bonfield is drawing near. His official days are numbered. His brutal assumption of authority, his clubbing exploits, his reception of presents from courtesans, gamblers, and saloonkeepers. His protection to disreputables will soon be a thing of the past. When that time comes it will be a glorious result for the city of Chicago. People do not want to be terrorizied; they want to be protected in their lives and liberty and property. Bonfield may as well prepare to retire to private life. Chicago has had enough of him and his methods."

89. TEUTONIA BUILDING AND FORMER SITE OF THE OFFICES OF THE ARBEITER-ZEITUNG (Southeast corner of Wells and Washington)

The Teutonia Building also shows the German character of Wells Street and it still stands at the southeast corner of Wells and Washington, but it has been completely modernized and now looks like a new building. In the modernization the Teutonia Building was extended at the rear, south along Wells, and it now occupies the site of the former offices of the Arbeiter-Zeitung.

The offices of The Arbeiter-Zeitung, edited by August Spies, and The Alarm, edited by Albert Parsons, were at 41 N. Wells. The German worker paper the Fackel was also printed here.

The building at 41 N. Wells (formerly 107 Fifth Ave.) was the center of many of the activities leading to the Haymarket Affair, since this was the center of communication for the workers of Chicago.

On April 28, 1885 thousands of people gathered in front of this building to protest the opening of the new $1,800,000 Board of Trade Building on LaSalle and Jackson. Parsons and Fielden spoke here protesting the $20 per plate dinner that was to be held by the rich that night at the dedication of the new building. The Socialists had decided to demonstrate against the tremendous cost of this building at a time when many were starving as the result of the depression which had started in 1882. Parsons said:

"The Board of Trade is a robbers' roost, and they are reveling on the proceeds of the workingman. How many of my hearers could give twenty dollars for supper tonight? We will never gain any-

The offices of the Alarm and Arbeiter-Zeitung on Wells Street.

thing by arguments and words. While those men are enjoying a sumptuous supper, workingmen are starving."

Samuel Fielden also spoke saying that the Board of Trade Building had been built out of money robbed from the workingmen since these men artificially fixed the prices of bread and other goods.

After the speeches, Oscar Neebe, Lucy Parsons, Lizzie Holmes and the others led a march up LaSalle Street, but the parade was intercepted by the Chicago Police Department under the direction of a Col. Walter.

It was in this building on May 3, 1886 that Spies wrote the flyer protesting the slaughter of workers at the McCormick Reaper Plant earlier that afternoon. On the next morning May 4, it was here that Fischer and Spies printed the flyer announcing the Haymarket Meeting.

On the evening of May 4, Lucy Parsons and Lizzie Holmes held their meeting of clothing workers to which Albert Parsons had also come. Albert later told what happened here that evening:

"When I got down there I found four or five other ladies there, and about—well, probably, twelve or fifteen—men. It was about 8:30 o'clock when we opened . . . We stayed about half an hour. We settled the business. About the time we were through

Wells Street looking north from Monroe at about the time of the Martyrs' funeral. Notice the print shops, clothing companies, and the absence of the elevated tracks. (Courtesy of Chicago Historical Society)

with it a committee came from the Haymarket saying: 'Nobody is over there but Spies. There is an awful big crowd, 3,000 or 4,000 people. For God's sake send somebody over. Come over, Parsons: come over, Fielden.' Well, we went there . . . "

Everyone went downstairs to the restaurant-saloon on the first floor and waited for a few minutes while little Albert and Lulu had a drink of water, and then they all rushed down Washington Street through the tunnel under the river and on to Haymarket Square.

On the morning of May 5, 1886, it was here that Captain Bonfield arrested Fischer and Spies and closed down all the workingmen's newspapers. That afternoon during a second raid they found Oscar Neebe at the office. He had just dropped by, and they arrested him too.

On Sunday, November 13, 1887 as the funeral procession passed this building, it was draped in black.

This building continued to be used by labor groups for many years, and in the 1920's the restaurant on the first floor was one of Clarence Darrow's favorite hang-outs. By the 1960's the restaurant had become a pizzeria, and then the building was demolished.

Across the street from this location were the offices for many years of Kerr and Co., which is still in existence. Kerr was the first publisher in America to publish the works of Karl Marx and Engels. Kerr later became the publishers for the Socialist Party and especially for the writings of Eugene Debs.

90. WELLS STREET CLOTHING AND WAREHOUSE DISTRICT

The funeral cortege continued up Wells Street toward the Grand Central Station at Harrison, and as they traveled south along Wells passing Adams, Quincy, Jackson, and Van Buren they passed many warehouses, clothing stores and factories.

Today some clothing plants and tailoring establishments still line the south end of Wells although they are fast disappearing as new high rise offices are being constructed.

Many Jewish workers toiled in these sweatshop factories seven days a week, and they turned out in great numbers to line Wells Street to mourn the deaths of the five Martyrs. Both Lucy and Albert Parsons had worked with these clothing workers helping them to organize.

The Grand Central Station from which the funeral trains departed for Waldheim Cemetery. (Courtesy Chicago Historical Society)

91. FORMER SITE OF GRAND CENTRAL STATION
(Wells and Harrison Streets)

Although you will turn right now onto W. Congress Parkway and the Eisenhower Expressway, you will see ahead of you a large open area that was once the site of the Wisconsin Central Station, later known as the Grand Central Station. It was here that the funeral procession ended, but 30 special railroad cars were waiting to take the families and friends of the Martyrs the 10 miles to Waldheim Cemetery in Forest Park, Illinois. Eventually over 10,000 people traveled out to the cemetery for the burial, many going by carriage. The train followed the same route as the Eisenhower Expressway.

At the time of the funeral, the Grand Central Station was under construction, but the railroad sheds at the back were completed. The new station was not officially dedicated until December of 1890. The beautiful station building was designed ironically by Solon Beman who had in 1880 built the town of Pullman for George Pullman, whose object was to remove his employees from the evil influence of Chicago and the anarchist labor agitators.

Between 1971 and 1972, Beman's beautiful red brick station with its 242 foot clock tower was demolished. This entire area is now to be the site for a new planned residential community.

92. "LITTLE ITALY," HULL HOUSE, AND THE UNIVERSITY OF ILLINOIS AT CHICAGO CIRCLE

Although you are traveling the same route followed by the funeral train in 1887 as you drive west on the Eisenhower, the scene has changed greatly. The Circle Campus of the University of Illinois on your left has replaced a large section of "Little Italy" and other ethnic communities that once existed here.

It was from a hall on Green Street and Harrison on May 5, 1886 (now the site of the Art and Architecture Building at Circle) that Jewish clothing workers tried to lead a march into the downtown area to protest rats, garbage and bad housing. They didn't know that martial law had been declared after Haymarket and they were met by police at the Van Buren Street Bridge and clubbed, beaten, and driven back to the westside of the river. Then the bridges were raised to protect the city from the Jews.

On your left a short distance up Halsted Street, Jane Addams, in October of 1889, opened Hull House. Jane Addams was called a do-gooder and a troublemaker when she tried to help the citizens of this community to organize unions and stand up for their rights. When she and the others at Hull House tried to end child labor, fight government corruption, and provide rights and equal pay for women, the same people who persecuted Parsons and the other Haymarket Martyrs began to persecute Hull House as well.

Jane Addams' friend and fellow social worker, Dr. Alice Hamilton, said that Hull House had a difficult time because the newspapers and prominent citizens always pointed to Haymarket and were suspect of anyone working with the poor.

However, the 98 lb. "Dr. Alice" fought on. She was beaten on the picket lines in the Clothing Workers' Strike of 1910. Two young people who attended programs at Hull House, Bessie Abramowitz and Sidney Hillman, would later help to found the Amalgamated Clothing Workers.

93. MIDWEST HEADQUARTERS OF THE AMALGAMATED CLOTHING WORKERS (Northeast corner of Ashland and Van Buren)

A mile further down the Eisenhower, on your right at Ashland Avenue, is a gray limestone building with a high tower. This is the Midwest Headquarters of the Amalgamated Clothing Workers Union that was founded at Hull House. This beautiful building was built in the early 1920's and contains large meeting rooms dedicated to the memories of Eugene Debs, Abraham Lincoln, and John Kennedy. Ground was broken for the building by Sidney Hillman, then President of the Amalgamated.

Today this building contains a center for Senior Citizens, a medical center, an insurance company, and a day-care center is next door. This union is also affiliated with a housing project on the Chicago southside and with a bank.

The clothing workers of Chicago have come a long way since Lucy Parsons' meeting at the offices of the Arbeiter-Zeitung on the evening of May 4, 1886.

94. "UNION ROW," FORMER SITE OF THE ASHLAND AUDITORIUM, AND TEAMSTER CITY (Along Ashland Avenue)

Ashland Avenue is sometimes known as "Union Row" because so many union headquarters line this street. Once located in the downtown area, high real estate values forced many unions to move to the westside and into this old mansion area.

First these mansions were converted to union offices, and later the original buildings were demolished and new buildings were built for the specific needs of the different unions.

The great Ashland Auditorium or Carmen's Hall once stood across the street from the Amalgamated Clothing Workers on the northwest corner of Ashland and Van Buren. This hall was built by the Amalgamated Transit Workers Union Division 241 that had been fought by Charles Yerkes, "The Streetcar King", and Captain Bonfield at the time of the Streetcar Strike of 1885. The Ashland Auditorium was a huge auditorium built in 1918 at a cost of $600,000. It was built in a "French Style" with a mansard roof at the top of its 4 stories. It was torn down in 1966 because the building was losing money. A service station now occupies the site with a sign giving the time and weather report.

It was here that a great debate took place between William Z. Foster (See No. 116) and Earl Howard Dean in 1922 on "Communism vs. Capitalism" and 4,000 people filled the auditorium to hear them.

"Teamster City" (330 Ashland), a modern, square, glass curtain wall type building opened in Feb. 1970, is the newest addition to "Union Row." It cost $3 million to build.

95. THE VILLAGE OF OAK PARK, THE FORMER HOME OF JUROR HARRY T. SANDFORD (Between Austin and Harlem on the Eisenhower)

Eight miles west of downtown Chicago, you come to the suburb of Oak Park which was once known as "The Middle-Class Capital of the World." This was once the home of Frank Lloyd Wright, who built dozens of beautiful homes here. Edgar Rice Burroughs lived here, and he thought up many of the Tarzan Stories in his plush home on Oak Park Avenue. Ernest Hemingway left Oak Park after World War I and moved to the northside, and later he moved to Paris because he hated the narrow middle-class attitude then shown by this community. But today Oak Park is an integrated, liberal, and forward looking community.

Oak Park had still another citizen of historical importance, Harry T. Sandford, the last of the jurors selected in the Haymarket Trial. In 1886, he was 25 years old and a junior executive with the Northwestern Railroad.

When the Illinois Supreme Court reviewed the case on whether the jury was properly selected, the only two jurors whose selection was examined were Theodore Denker and Harry T. Sandford.

Sandford had admitted that he had already formed and expressed an opinion as to the guilt of the accused and he declared that he was prejudiced against the defendants.

Under the persuasive questioning of Judge Gary, however, Sandford stated that he "believed" he could render a fair and impartial verdict. He was challenged for cause by the attorney of the Haymarket Eight, but Judge Gary promptly overruled the challenge, and Sandford became the twelfth juror.

Because of Sandford and other injustices during the trial, the defense lawyer, Captain Black, appealed the case and instead of being hung on Dec. 3, 1886, the Haymarket Eight were spared until a Supreme Court decision could be made. It finally came on September 14, 1887, after months of delay, but the verdict was upheld and the hanging rescheduled for Nov. 11, 1887. It is interesting historically, however, that after this trial, new laws were passed for the selection of jurors. But this was too late for the Haymarket Martyrs.

NOTE: Exit left at Harlem Avenue off the Eisenhower Expressway, turn left again at the top of the ramp onto Harlem Avenue, and then right at the very next light onto Harrison Street.

96. THE TOWN OF FOREST PARK AND ST. BERNARDINE CHURCH AND SCHOOL (Southwest corner of Harrison and Elgin)

You are now in Forest Park, Illinois, one of the older suburbs of Chicago. This community was originally part of the Harlem Community organized by German settlers in the later 1840's as a farm community and named after Haarlem in the Netherlands.

The north end of Forest Park is still filled with German restaurants, a large German Old People's Home, and a few German beer gardens. Each year the community still celebrates "Octoberfest," and one of the Protestant churches still presents a Sunday morning worship service in German.

As Anglo-Saxon Protestant businessmen, who were anti-drinking, settled in the far north end of what was the original community a debate developed between the new comers and the German farmers. The wealthier suburban settlers went to court and won, thus forming a new "dry" village which is now River Forest.

As Italians from "Little Italy" (See No. 92) could afford to move westward out of the ghetto, Forest Park proved ideal since it was directly west and convenient to the Congress "L" line. Therefore south Forest Park became a very Italian community, and you will see many Italian names on the businesses in this area.

St. Bernardine Church, built in a beautiful Italian-Spanish style of yellow brick and stone, illustrates the ethnic mix of Forest Park. If you wish, stop and look at the plaque and World War II marker in front of the church at the southwest corner of Harrison and Elgin.

The church was built in 1939 under Monsignor John T. Wagener, a German, who was the pastor from 1935-1967. But the World War II marker gives the names of men from the parish who fought in this war, and they include English, German and Italian names, such as Kern, Iovino, Obermayer, and Lentini.

Forest Park is also the home of German Waldheim (Forest Home) Cemetery, the only cemetery in the Chicago area for many years that practiced no racial, political, or ethnic discrimination in regard to who could be buried here. This would be the only cemetery willing to receive the remains of the Haymarket Martyrs.

97. PARK DISTRICT OF FOREST PARK (Along northside of Harrison Street from Hannah Street to DesPlaines)

Continue driving west on Harrison Street and soon you will see on your right a beautiful park.

After the Panic of 1873 and the numerous depressions of the 1880's, the Workingmen's Parties of Illinois and others throughout the nation asked the local, state, and federal governments for public jobs. This type of public service employment was something that Lucy and Albert Parsons had often marched for. However, it would not be until the Depression of the 1930's and Roosevelt's New Deal that unemployed workers would be given work on government funded projects. This beautiful park and the buildings in it are an example of the worthwhile projects built under the Works Progress Administration (WPA).

This park was built between 1936 and 1938. It contains a beautiful stone "Tudor Style" community center, tennis courts, and one of the finest swimming pools in West Suburban Chicago. Later, between 1967 and 1973 the Village of Forest Park made additional improvements such as a children's playground, horseshoe courts, shuffleboard, and a ballfield. Not only did this project provide employment for workers of the 1930's, but it is now providing recreation and a better life for their children and grandchildren; and it will do the same for generations to come.

98. FOREST HOME OR GERMAN WALDHEIM CEMETERY (Along DesPlaines Just South of Harrison)

When you reach Des Plaines turn left and travel a short distance. You will see the cemetery at your right; turn right through the gate.

Originally this cemetery was incorporated on March 13, 1875 as German Waldheim. The first interment took place on July 16, 1874. This cemetery is only one of many ethnic cemeteries in Forest Park. Over 350,000 graves are contained in Jewish Waldheim (south of Roosevelt Road), German Waldheim, Concordia, Forest Home (west of the DesPlaines River), and several other small cemeteries. People jokingly describe Forest Park (population 15,000) as "more dead than alive."

This area was once the burial grounds of the Potawatomi Indians, and the high ground of this cemetery was once an Indian trial running along the DesPlaines River. But with the building of the Chicago and Northwestern Railroad and the

Aurora, Elgin and Chicago Railroad, which ran parallel to the present Eisenhower Expressway, the area became accessible as a cemetery for the thousands of immigrants living in Chicago whose deceased were not welcomed in the Chicago cemeteries. With the building of a streetcar line on DesPlaines Street, each Saturday and Sunday thousands of people could come out to these cemeteries by train, transfer to the streetcar, and buy flowers from the many nurseries in the area to place on the graves of their loved ones.

Over 2,500 graves had to be moved from German Waldheim when the Eisenhower Expressway was built in the 1950's. The law required the permission of all known descendants who were notified by registered letter or public notice in the newspapers. This delayed completion of this part of the Eisenhower for several years.

A plaque on the gate house and flower shop building gives dates when the cemetery was reorganized (1881), and rebuilt (1905). It was renamed "Forest Home" in about 1973, which is simply the English meaning of the German word "Waldheim."

On the afternoon of the same day as the Haymarket Affair, Tuesday, May 4, Samuel Fielden, in his wagon which was for hire, brought to this cemetery a load of gravel for the very roadbeds you are now driving on. Little did Fielden realize that all his friends would soon be buried here.

99. HAYMARKET MARTYRS' MONUMENT

After passing the cemetery flowershop veer to the left toward the beautiful cream-colored stone "Norman Styled" Chapel of the cemetery. Opposite the Chapel is the Haymarket Martyrs' Monument. Park along the road and walk through the remaining sites on this tour.

This beautiful monument was designed by the sculptor, Albert Weinert. Justice is represented by a woman placing a laurel wreath on the head of a fallen worker. She is marching into the future, ready to draw the sword if she must, to win a better life for the generations to come.

The sculptor was inspired to use this theme because the Haymarket Martyrs had sung the "Marseillaise", the French national anthem written at the time of the French Revolution. One of the verses of the song described the scene you see here.

We have now completed the retracing of the funeral route of Sunday, November 13, 1887. The 30 special railroad cars stopped just to the north of the cemetery where today the Chicago Transit Authority surface line ends. The coffins were then carried into the cemetery and thousands of people gathered around this spot.

The bodies of Spies, Parsons, Engel, Fischer, and Lingg were placed in a simple temporary vault as everyone listened to their attorney, William Black, give his eulogy just as the sun was setting.

In the years between 1887 and 1893, Lucy Parsons worked hard to set up the Pioneer Aid and Support Association to provide for the widows and orphans of those who were executed as well as the dependents of those who were still in Joliet penitentiary. This society also supported publications on the Haymarket case, as well as appeals for the freeing of those still in jail. It was the Pioneer Aid and Support Association that erected this monument, especially important after the erection of the Police Monument in Haymarket Square (See No. 8).

When this monument was dedicated another parade was held in downtown Chicago, with a ceremony here on Sunday, June 25, 1893. Marching in this second parade were over 3,000 people including singing societies, Turners, trade unionists, and musical organizations. Thousands of people watched the 1893 parade as it went up Market Street (now South Wacker Drive), then east to Wells and south to Harrison where five special trains, again at the Grand Central Station, were waiting to carry the throng to this spot. The Chicago Tribune, usually conservative in its estimates of crowds, reported that over 8,000 people went out to the cemetery after the parade. The Columbian Exposition was taking place at this time and there were visitors in Chicago from all over the world, many of whom came out here that day.

When the thousands arrived here an interesting program was planned with speeches in English, German, Bohemian, and Polish. There were floral tributes from unions in England, France, and Belgium. The monument was draped in red, and the speakers platform was decorated with the crimson banner of the Architectural Ironworkers Union No. 2, the blue flag of the Brewery Workers Union, the red banners of the International Mannerchor and of the Workingmen's Clubs, and the Stars and Stripes.

The "Red Squad" of the Chicago Police Department was here, and the Tribune reported that "detectives from the Chicago force mingled with the throngs and a photographer quietly took several views of those around the platform."

The program began with the sculptor, Weinert, presenting the statue to the President of the Pioneer Aid and Support Association. Fetzner's Orchestra played the "Marseillaise," and the monument was unveiled by Albert Parsons Jr., then 14 years of age. The Humboldt Singing Society sang an old Lutheran hymn, "Wake Up," and then Dr. Ernest Schmidt spoke. Dr. Schmidt, one of the most distinguished physicians in Chicago and a neighbor, ironically, of George Pullman, had once run as a Socialist candidate for Mayor of Chicago. He was also a leader in the movement for the pardon of Fielden, Schwab and Neebe.

Seventy-eight years later on Sunday, May 2, 1971, the ceremony was repeated as Irving Abrams, a Chicago attorney and the last surviving member of the Pioneer Aid and Support Society, presented the deed to the monument to the Illinois Labor History Society, in the presence of Mark Neebe, a great grandson of Oscar Neebe. A student from Concordia Teachers College Choir of the nearby German Lutheran school in River Forest sang "Wake Up" and the "Marseillaise." Joseph Jacobs, the labor attorney, again read from Dr. Schmidt's 1893 address.

Each year, on the Sunday closest to May 4th, members of the Illinois Labor History Society and other organizations gather here to say a few words and to place red roses and a wreath at the foot of the monument. Red roses were carried at the original funeral, placed here at the original dedication of this monument, and they have become a symbol of these men who died for freedom of speech and assembly.

Other organizations place wreaths here on November 11th each year; "Black Friday," the day that Parsons, Engel, Fischer, and Spies were executed.

At the base of the statue are the last words spoken by August Spies.

On the afternoon of November 22, 1895, Eugene Debs came here after having been released from Woodstock Jail, where he had served six months for leading the Pullman Strike. Debs stood in front of this monument and prayed silently. He came directly here before going to be greeted by half a million workers in downtown Chicago.

On the day after the dedication of this monument, June 26, 1893 Governor John Peter Altgeld not only pardoned Schwab, Neebe and Fielden but condemned the police, the judge, the jury, the state's attorney, and the entire judicial system that had conspired to execute the martyrs for their ideas. If you walk around the back of the monument you will see part of the pardon message. It was added later to the monument.

Biographical information on all of the Haymarket Eight will not be included here since five of them were discussed earlier. (For Louis Lingg see No. 45; for Albert Parsons see No. 48; August Spies see No. 63; for Adolph Fischer see No. 71; for George Engel see No. 79). However, following are short biographical sketches of Michael Schwab, Oscar Neebe, and Samuel Fielden.

MICHAEL SCHWAB was 32 years old at the time of the Haymarket Affair. He was an editorial writer for the Arbeiter-Zeitung and helped edit the flyer written by Spies after the attack by Bonfield on the workers at the McCormick Plant.

On the evening of May 4, 1886 he dropped by the Haymarket meeting for a few minutes around 8:00 p.m., but could not stay since he had been invited to speak that night to hundreds of workers at the Deering Harvester Plant on Clybourn. The organizing committee at Deering invited him to have a beer after the meeting. He then took a streetcar on Clybourn back to his home near North Avenue. It was 11:00 p.m. when he returned home, half an hour after the bomb was thrown. He was about three miles away at the time of the explosion.

Schwab had served nearly six years of a life sentence in Joliet penitentiary at the time Altgeld pardoned him. When he returned home on the evening of June 26, 1893, he found his wife well but his two children very ill with scarlet fever. Although there were numerous receptions and musical concerts that took place at Grief's Hall and the offices of the Arbeiter-Zeitung to celebrate the release of the men, Schwab did not go with Neebe and Fielden to these functions. He at first resumed his position as an editorial writer on the Arbeiter-Zeitung, but he quarrelled with its directors and resigned in 1895.

Schwab then opened a shoe store at Belmont and North Paulina, where he carried shoes and a stock of books. This business failed, and he became ill; he was supported in the last years of his life by the Pioneer Aid and Support Society and by his good friend Eugene Dietzgen, the drawing material company owner. He died of pneumonia, which he had contracted at Joliet Penitentiary, in the Alexian Brothers Hospital at the age of 45 on June 29, 1898. He left a wife and four children, two of whom were born after his return from prison.

One of the children born after his release was named Johanna Altgeld Schwab in honor of Governor John Peter Altgeld. Johanna Altgeld Schwab grew up in San Francisco and became a social worker. She and her husband Dr. Milton

Thorpe became noted humanitarians and were responsible for the escape of many Jews from Germany during the Hitler era.

OSCAR NEEBE was born in New York City on July 12, 1850, but his parents immigrated back to Hesse Cassel, Germany so that Neebe would have a German education. He returned to the United States when he was 14 years old as the Civil War was drawing to a close.

He first worked as a gold and silver beater in Houston, N.Y., and then at the age of 16 came to Chicago where he found himself broke, with no place to live, and only 40¢ in his pocket. He bought some bread and a newspaper with his remaining money, and found a job through an advertisement with the Lake House saloon on Rush Street. He worked for Mr. and Mrs. Martin Keller who were very kind to him from 1866 to 1868. This saloon was frequented by many of the McCormick Reaper workers, since the original plant had been near the mouth of the Chicago River before the Great Fire. Neebe learned of the problems of the workers as he talked with them in the saloon.

Later he moved to Cleveland, then to New York where he became a tinsmith. In Philadelphia visiting his brother in 1873 he met his first wife Meta, and they came to Chicago again in February, 1877. Neebe worked for the Adams' Westlake Manufacturing Company but when he tried to organize the workers he was "blacklisted." The period from 1877 to 1879 was very difficult, but he finally got another job with the Riverdale Distilling Company selling yeast. In 1881, along with his brother and several partners he founded the Acme Yeast Company.

He read a great deal, especially the works of Jefferson and Thomas Paine. Neebe became involved with various worker groups, and in 1880 he contributed money to the Socialistic Publishing Company that later published the Arbeiter-Zeitung. He also was active with the Central Labor Unions of Chicago.

When he was arrested on May 5, 1886, he was told by State's Attorney Grinnell that a few prominent German brewers had told Grinnell he was a dangerous man. Since Neebe had helped to organize the brewery workers and gain higher wages for them, then one can see why many of the brewers might have considered Neebe a danger.

His first wife died while he was imprisoned, leaving two girls and a boy. His children were cared for by his brother until his pardon in 1893. He later remarried. The William Neebe who designed the cover and maps for this book is Oscar Neebe's grandchild by this second marriage.

Oscar Neebe lived quietly after his pardon and he ran a Chicago tavern for a number of years. He died at his residence at 1717 Hammond at the age of 65 on April 22, 1916. He was then buried like Schwab beside this monument.

SAMUEL FIELDEN and Parsons were the only two of the Haymarket Eight that were not German. Fielden was born on February 25, 1847 in Lancashire, England. His childhood in England was straight out of a Dickens' novel, working long hours at the looms with little or no education. His mother died when he was only ten.

Between the ages of 18 and 21, Fielden became very active in the work of the Methodist Church and as a local preacher he would circuit ride from town to town. He combined the religious faith of his mother with the political action of his father, and was often told by church officials that he was too worldly.

In July, 1868 he left England for the United States and arrived in New York with only $15 in his pocket. He worked in Brooklyn but decided to come west to Chicago in August of 1869. Later he traveled through the South and was shocked by the system of sharecropping used to enslave the Blacks after the Civil War.

In 1871, he again returned to Chicago where he worked dredging the Sag Canal as well as working for former Mayor Wentworth on his farm at Summit-Argo. He lived for a while in Lawndale, but in 1886 he was living on Polk Street near Jefferson.

He married in 1880 and had a son and daughter at the time of the Haymarket Affair. Everyone knew him as "Good-natured Sam."

Like Parsons it was a strange twist of fate that he was speaking on Desplaines Street when the bomb was thrown. When he left his house on Polk Street he just intended to address Lucy's meeting of clothing workers and then come home.

After his release from prison he remained in Chicago for awhile. Someone who greatly admired him left him a ranch in La'Veta, Colorado. Fielden died at this ranch on February 7, 1922 at the age of 75. It seems Fielden is the only one of the Haymarket Eight not to be buried here. He was probably buried at La Veta, although county records do not show this.

100. GRAVE OF LUCY PARSONS (1853-1942)

Under this small, simple stone lie the remains of a great and brave woman, who fought for women's rights, union organization, and civil rights.

She was born in Johnson County, Texas about 1853, and was of Black, Spanish, and Indian ancestry. The truth about her early background is somewhat of a mystery. In later years, the Rosser family claimed she was their former slave, Malinda, who left them after the Civil War in Houston, Texas. There were also numerous stories that she was previously married in Texas; but none of these stories was ever proved and the newspapers used them as a way of discrediting her.

Although Republicans in the South, Lucy and Albert found the Republican Party in Chicago hostile to ethnic, minority, and racial groups and their problems when they came here about 1873. Therefore, by 1877 they had become members of the Socialistic Labor Party. When Albert ran for several different city offices, Lucy assisted in his campaign. She also became a leading writer for The Alarm.

Lucy wrote articles protesting the Lemont Massacre in May of 1885, and was the standard bearer during the march against the opening of the new Board of Trade Building. Lucy spoke at numerous Lake Front Park (Grant Park) rallies, led the Thanksgiving Day "Poor People's March" in 1884, and marched with Albert and her children at the head of 80,000 workers on May 1, 1886.

After Albert was found guilty, Lucy started on a cross-country speaking tour to tell the true story of Haymarket. Later she went to Europe and spoke in London where George Bernard Shaw and Oscar Wilde had taken up the cause of the Haymarket Eight.

Lucy went out on the streets of Chicago and sold 5,000 copies, at five cents, of General Trumbull's pamphlet "Was It A Fair Trial? An Appeal to the Governor of Illinois." She was constantly arrested by the police. After her husband's execution she prepared the book, "The Life of Albert R. Parsons," in 1889, and she dedicated the book to Albert by saying, "This Book is Lovingly Dedicated to the Sacred Memory of one whose only crime was that he lived in advance of his time . . . ."

Her life was one tragedy after another. Her children Lulu and

Lucy Parsons in 1886

Albert Jr. both died young and their remains were cremated. She kept them close to her in her home at 3130 North Troy.

For the rest of Lucy's life she worked for social justice, and in 1905 was at the founding convention of the Industrial Workers of the World. At that convention she predicted the 1930's "sit-in strike" of the CIO, when she said:

"My conception of the strike of the future is not to strike and go out and starve, but to strike and remain in and take possession of the necessary property of production . . . ."

Her love life was also tragic. After the death of Albert and her daughter Lulu she was very lost, but threw herself into writing and fighting for the pardoning of the others. A young worker fell in love with her but he was unstable, and beat her and broke all the furniture in her house. In the early 1900's she supposedly had a brief love affair with Dr. Ben Reitman (See No. 105), who was Emma Goldman's young protege (See No. 120); and this caused some bitterness between Emma and Lucy for the rest of their lives. From about 1910 until her tragic death in 1942 she lived with George Markshall.

Lucy would become a familiar sight in every radical march during the 1920's and 1930's.

Her house caught on fire on the afternoon of Saturday, March

7, 1942. Since she was blind by then she could not get out of the building. George Markshall tried to save her but he was overcome by the smoke and eventually also died from the fire.

She had asked to be buried here next to her first husband, and she was cremated and buried here along with the ashes of Lulu and Albert Jr. that she had always kept close to her. The ashes of George Markshall, who had loved and looked after her in her later years, are also buried in this same grave.

Her extensive library of 2,500 to 3,000 volumes along with many letters was only slightly damaged by the fire, but they mysteriously disappeared. Many people believed they were taken by the "Red Squad" of the Police Department.

Lucy willed her house and the land it stood on to the Pioneer Aid and Support Association, and what remained was sold so that the Martyrs' Monument could be preserved.

In 1976, the Charles H. Kerr Publishing Company published a book entitled "Lucy Parsons: American Revolutionary," by Carolyn Ashbaugh and finally the whole story of the life of this extraordinary woman is again being told.

101. GRAVE OF VOLTAIRINE DE CLEYRE (1866-1912)

Voltairine De Cleyre was named by her father after the philosopher Voltaire. Voltairine spent four years in a convent, but rebelled against that life and fled to Philadelphia and later Baltimore, where she taught English to immigrant workers.

When the Haymarket bomb exploded in Chicago and the eight men were arrested, Voltairine said, "They ought to be hanged!" Fifteen years later she confessed:

"For that ignorant, outrageous, bloodthirsty sentence I shall never forgive myself, though I know the dead men would have forgiven me, though I know those who loved them forgive me."

Voltairine said that until the Haymarket Trial, she had always believed in the "essential justice" of the "American law" and trial by jury, but "after this I never could," she said.

When Leon Czolgosz, a supposed anarchist, but actually a mentally disturbed young man, killed President McKinley in 1901, Senator R. Hawley said, "I have an utter abhorrence of anarchy and would give a thousand dollars to get a good shot at an anarchist." The Nation magazine feared that if Senator Hawley's hand were no steadier than his mind, an anarchist could pick up an easy thousand dollars.

Voltairine offered herself as a target to Hawley, provided he would first give her a few minutes to explain "anarchism" to him. However, the Senator never accepted her offer.

When Voltairine was one of the main speakers at the Cooper Union in New York against police censorship she said the following to 2,000 people:

"Freedom of speech means nothing if it does not mean the freedom for that to be said which we do not like."

Emma Goldman was a good friend and she said the following in her autobiography:

"On my return East I learned of the death . . . Her end affected me very deeply: her whole life had been a continuous chain of suffering. Death had come after an operation for an abcess on the brain which had impaired her memory. A second operation would have deprived her of the power of speech. Voltairine,

always stoical in pain, preferred death. Her end, on June 19, was a great loss.

Arriving in Chicago, I went out to Waldheim with Annie Livshis, a dear friend . . . I went to the cemetery with red carnations in my arms, while Annie carried red geraniums to be added to those she had already planted on the fresh grave. These were the only monument Voltairine had ever wanted . . . .

As I stood beside Voltairine's grave, in the shadow of the monument dedicated to the memory of our comrades, I felt that another martyr had been added to them. She was the prototype of the sculptured Waldheim figure, beautiful in her spiritual defiance and filled with the revolt of a flaming ideal."

Voltairine's ideas still live on in her book of essays and poems, "Selected Works of Voltairine De Cleyre," first published in 1914 and reissued by the Revisionist Press in 1972. Among her poems are many connected with Haymarket: "John P. Altgeld," "Light Upon Waldheim," "At the Grave at Waldheim," and "In Memoriam—To Gen. M. M. Trumbull."

102. GRAVE OF META NEEBE

This is the grave of the first wife of Oscar Neebe who died as a result of the anguish of the Haymarket Trial and the imprisonment in Joliet of her husband. She died on March 11, 1887 and a large funeral service was held for her in Mueller's Hall (See No. 44). She was originally buried in another cemetery, then moved later after her husband, Oscar Neebe, was buried here.

103. GRAVE OF HARRY KELLY (1871-1953)

Harry Kelly was a writer and educator. He was a founder of the Ferrer Modern School in Stelton, New Jersey, and he wrote articles for Emma Goldman's monthly magazine Mother Earth, which began publication in March of 1906.

Kelly had been an associate of Prince Kropotkin at the time of his tour of the United States when he spoke at Hull House. Emma Goldman always referred to Kropotkin as her true teacher and inspiration.

Kelly offered to marry Emma to prevent her from being deported by J. Edgar Hoover and Attorney-General Palmer under the Alien and Sedition Act in 1919. He had hoped by marrying her to make her American citizenship unquestionable. Emma refused to let Kelly do this and she was deported.

When Emma Goldman returned to the U.S. for the only other time in her life during March of 1935, Kelly was there to greet her. He and Emma attended a reception for her at the Waldorf-Astoria Hotel sponsored by Roger Baldwin of the American Civil Liberties Union. John Dewey, the educator, also came along with 300 other guests, an additional 500 were turned away.

104. GRAVE OF ANN SOSNOVSKY WINOKUR

Ann Winokur was an early member of the International Ladies Garment Workers Union (ILGWU). This union was organized in New York City in 1900, and celebrated its 75th Anniversary in 1975.

The ILGWU was involved in a number of great strikes throughout the United States in 1909, 1910, and 1913. Today the Chicago offices of the ILGWU are located near the site of the old Market Square where Parsons often spoke. In the building at 15 S. Wacker Drive they have educational facilities, a health center, an insurance service, and many social services for their members.

Ann Winokur's daughter also became an active member of the union and the Winokur family still live in the Chicago area.

105. GRAVE OF DR. BEN REITMAN (1880-1942)

This is the grave of one of Emma Goldman's many lovers. Reitman was born in St. Paul, Minnesota. His peddler father and his mother deserted him when he was only a few years old.

When he was eight he was a "pimp" running errands for prostitutes in the slum and vice area near the Polk Street Station. At eleven he ran away from home and worked as a sailor traveling around the world. At seventeen he was converted to Baptist Revival Christianity in a Bowery Mission. At nineteen he took a job as a janitor in the Chicago Polyclinic. Some doctors took an interest in him, and they helped him make a startling jump from a fourth grade education to medical school. Then, as Reitman said, I "somehow passed medical school and the state board examination."

By 1910 Dr. Reitman had become an eccentric Chicago physician. Dr. Reitman became the most conspicuous figure in the International Itinerant Migratory Workers' Union, or the Hobos of America, Inc. Reitman was known across the country as the "King of the Hobos" and he even founded an early workers' education school called Hobo College in a storefront on Madison Street. Emma first met Dr. Reitman when he let her speak at Hobo College in 1910 to a gathering of transients and unemployed men. Although Emma was 41 at the time and Reitman only 30, they fell in love. Reitman eventually became Emma's tour manager. Whenever Emma spoke, Dr. Reitman also gave a speech on his favorite topic, the treatment of veneral disease.

It is difficult to describe "Dr. Ben." Emma described him as tall, with a finely shaped head which was covered by a mass of black curls—his curls, unfortunately, like his fingernails were successful fugitives from soap and water.

Margaret Anderson, an associate of Emma Goldman, always said that "the fantastic Dr. Ben Reitman . . . wasn't so bad if you could hastily drop all your ideas as to how human beings should look or act."

Emma would always reply, "Hobo will learn." She later wrote that she knew him "inside out" in two weeks. She "loathed his sensational ways, bombast, braggadocio . . . his promiscuity which lacked the least sense of selection," but she said "there was something large, primitive, and unpremeditated about Ben which had terrific charm." Reitman always called Emma his "Blue-Eyed Mommy."

In May of 1914, Reitman and Emma went to San Diego to take part in a "free speech rally" after city officials had passed an ordinance to forbid outdoor oratory.

When they reached their hotel the Mayor of San Diego and the Chief of Police talked with Emma and told her it was too dangerous for her to give a speech. While she was talking with the city officials, Reitman disappeared. Later in the day Reitman turned up in Los Angeles, a pitiable sight.

Armed men had forced Reitman to accompany them twenty miles south of San Diego. There vigilantes tarred and, in lieu of feathers, sage-brushed him.

"We could tear your guts out," Reitman later recalled them saying, "but we promised the Chief of Police not to kill you."

He was brutally beaten, one of the vigilantes used a lighted cigar to burn the letters IWW on his buttocks. This painful ceremony concluded on a patriotic note when he was forced to kiss the flag and sing "The Star-Spangled Banner." Reitman insisted on returning again and again to San Diego until Emma was finally allowed to speak in 1916.

When Emma was deported from the United States in 1919 and visited Russia, she became very disillusioned with Soviet Communism. Reitman disagreed with her and thought her too critical, and they gradually drifted apart.

In the 1920's Dr. Reitman was known as the "Reverend" of the Dill Pickle Club (See No. 35). He also wrote a great deal and took part in many marches. Reitman's papers, letters, and books are a part of the collection at the library at the University of Illinois at Chicago Circle.

He died suddenly in 1942, although he appeared in the picture of health. Irving Abrams, of the Pioneer Aid and Support Association, was asked by Reitman at Lucy Parsons' funeral in March if Irving would also give his eulogy when he died. Within the year Reitman was dead, and Irving Abrams again spoke.

106. GRAVE OF ELIZABETH JOHNSTONE (Died 1954)
Elizabeth Johnstone was the wife of Jack Johnstone (See No. 119). She outlived her husband some twelve years, but during his lifetime she assisted him in his work in this country and throughout the world. She also worked with the education department of the Communist Party of Illinois.

107. GRAVE OF FRANK MUCCI (1905-1954)
Born in central southern Illinois, Frank Mucci's parents came to America from Italy to work in the coal mining area just south of Springfield. Whole communities of Ukranians, Welsh, Irish, Italian, and Southern Blacks were brought into Illinois and played against each other by the mine owners in order to prevent unionization and higher wages. This brought about the Virden Massacre (1898) and later the Herrin Massacre (1922).

As a young boy Frank Mucci also became a miner, and a union organizer. Mucci has the unique distinction of being the first Communist to be elected to public office in the State of Illinois. He was elected to the City Council of his hometown, Taylor Springs, Illinois.

Mucci became a leader of the Progressive Mine Workers of America. It is the Progressive Miners' Cemetery at Mt. Olive, Illinois that contains the grave of "Mother Jones" who was buried here along with victims of the Virden Massacre.

In the 1940s, Frank Mucci was a leader of the split in the United Mine Workers against John L. Lewis. Mucci died in 1954 at the age of 49.

Frank Mucci's wife, Lois, is still alive. Before marrying Frank, Lois was married to a member of the "Lincoln Brigade" who died in Spain fighting against Franco Facism. Ernest Hemingway (See No. 36 and No. 95) also fought with this group and wrote about them in "For Whom the Bells Toll".

After Frank's death Lois married another member of the "Lincoln Brigade" and moved to California.

108. GRAVE OF ALFRED WAGENKNECHT (1881-1956)

Alfred Wagenknecht was known to William Z. Foster and his close friends as "Wag." In his early years he was a member of Eugene Debs' Socialist Party. He also helped to organize lumber workers in the State of Washington. Later he moved to Ohio and became the Secretary of the Socialist Party.

At the Socialist Convention in St. Louis in April 1917, Wagenknecht supported the resolution on World War I that stated that "this is not a war for freedom, but a war for profit." Wagenknecht was jailed for his opposition to the war. It was the defense of Alfred Wagenknechts' right to dissent in a speech given on June 16, 1918 that led to Eugene Debs' imprisonment.

When Wagenknecht and John Reed, who both represented the left wing of the Socialist Party, tried to attend the Socialist Convention in August of 1919 they were expelled. Angry, Reed, Wagenknecht, and 92 other expelled delegates formed the Communist Party of America on the next day, September 1, 1919.

During the Palmer Raids in Michigan in the 1920's, Wagenknecht was again arrested and thrown in jail for voicing his ideas. Wagenknecht supported two things that were later to become official government policy. First, as the head of an organization known as the Friends of Soviet Russia he raised money to send food to the Soviet Union during the early 1920's when millions were starving. Later, Herbert Hoover would head a government commission that would ship millions of tons of grain to Russia. Second, Wagenknecht wished the United States to recognize the Soviet Union and he gave speeches supporting this and was arrested. The United States would officially recognize the Soviet Union in 1934.

"Wag" was actively involved with the Trade Union Educational League (TUEL). He helped to organize workers in Passaic, New Jersey, and he was involved in the 11 month strike at the Botany Mills. During this strike at the Botany Mills, Wagenknecht got the AFL Bakers Union members on their own time, to bake free bread for the starving strikers. Elizabeth Gurley Flynn (See No. 155) and the women of the community took care of 1,000 strikers' children daily with free sandwiches and milk.

In May of 1931, he helped organize miners in Pennsylvania. In the 1930's he worked with the Chicago Federation of Labor to organize steel workers in Chicago. He was present at the Memorial Day Massacre in 1937.

109. GRAVE OF SAMUEL T. HAMMERSMARK (1872-1957)

Samuel Hammersmark was fourteen years old at the time of the Haymarket Affair, and he was shocked by the hanging and became an anarchist himself. In 1905, after the Industrial Workers of the World was formed, he became a member. Along with his friend William Z. Foster, he later became discouraged with the lack of effectiveness of the IWW, and he resigned. He and Foster then became active in the Syndicalist League of North America for the next two years.

Between 1917 and 1920 Hammersmark and Foster worked for the Chicago Federation of Labor organizing over a half million workers in the steel and meatpacking industries.

Working with his Black friend, James W. Ford, Hammersmark in the 1920's helped to organize the Post Office Workers Union in Chicago.

Hammersmark also worked with the Socialist Party and especially Congressman Berger of Wisconsin and his wife Matte who were his good friends. Later, Hammersmark became active with the Trade Union Educational League (TUEL), and he operated a bookstore for the League. He also worked closely with Jack Johnstone (See No. 119).

Samuel Hammersmark had known Lucy Parsons for many years, but during the last three years of Lucy's life they became very close and the two of them attended many rallies together.

His work with thousands of steelworkers and packinghouse workers alone makes the statement on his gravestone most appropriate . . . "He lived a life of service to mankind."

110. GRAVE OF FRANK A. PELLEGRINO (1890-1969) AND MORT SCHAFFNER (1953-1973)

Born in Italy, Frank Pellegrino came to the United States in 1905 when he was 15 years old. He came to Chicago, and here he worked in the garment factory area on the westside around Hull House. His understanding of both Italian and English made it possible for him to recruit many Italian workers, who were being used as strikebreakers, into the ranks of the Amalgamated Clothing Workers Union. Pellegrino was a Socialist at first, but as early as 1913 he joined the left wing of the party.

When World War I broke, Pellegrino refused to support the war and refused to buy Liberty Bonds. This resulted in his losing one job after another.

When the Communist Party started in Chicago in 1919, Frank Pellegrino became a charter member. He became a close friend of William Z. Foster.

In 1922, Pellegrino met and married Bessie, a Ukranian Jew, who was a supporter of Eugene Debs. Bessie was also a clothing worker. She had started working in a factory at 12 years of age along with her seven sisters and one brother for less than $3 a week. Bessie and Frank would be married for 47 years.

In the early 1920's, Sidney Hillman went to Russia to set up an American financed clothing plant under American management, but the Russians wanted their technicians to control the plant. This angered Hillman and he withdrew his offer to the Russians. This developed into a feud between Hillman and the leftist members of the Amalgamated Clothing Workers including Pellegrino.

Frank and Bessie Pellegrino went to Europe and Russia in 1967, and they hoped to go again on Frank's 80th birthday, but he died the year before. In the years before his death, Frank was busy collecting clippings and writing his autobiography, but it was never completed.

Before his death he had asked to be buried in Waldheim next to the Haymarket Martyrs. His son wished the words "Here lies a Communist" to appear on his grave, but his wife Bessie thought that people would say:

"When they are alive they are afraid . . . they say nothing . . . and when they die they place it on the grave."

The idea of the "hammer and sickle" was a compromise, since it tells us without words of his philosophy. However, the cemetery was not happy with this idea and according to Bessie the hammer and sickle more than doubled the cost of the cemetery marker.

MORT SCHAFFNER

About twenty-five steps further down the road, marked by a plaque very much like that of Frank Pellegrino, is the grave of one of the youngest persons to be buried here, Mort Schaffner, who died on Dec. 5, 1973 at the age of twenty.

Mort was a member of IBEW 1031. He ran in 1971 for the Niles Township School Board when he was 18 in order to challenge the law that minors couldn't run. After being ruled off the ballot, three weeks later the election code was amended making 18 year olds eligible.

While still in high school he fought for the re-instatement of four teachers that were fired for their political views and anti-Vietnam activities. He was a founding member and the Section Press Director of the Young Workers Liberation League of Illinois at the time of his death from a heart attack. His family which still lives in Skokie wished him buried here, representing a new generation of people working for social change.

111. GRAVE OF GERALDINE LIGHTFOOT (1912-1962)

Geraldine Lightfoot was born in Mississippi, but came to Chicago as a child. By the 1930's she had become one of the most active Black women in Chicago. She organized women on the south and west sides of the city, especially in the garment industry. She also worked with several Black churches. The words on her plaque are most appropriate . . . "Foremost fighter against race, national, and sex oppression."

Geraldine became the wife of Claude Lightfoot, for many years head of the Communist Party in the United States. She would continue to actively work with her husband until the late 1950's when she developed a brain tumor.

Geraldine was sent to a Chicago hospital and placed under the care of a German refugee doctor, who discovered her membership in the Communist Party when he was questioning her about her husband's profession. This doctor told Geraldine, in the presence of her husband Claude, that he would not care for her or operate on her because she was a Communist!

Claude Lightfoot, upset and crying, called his friend Jack Kling, who worked in Chicago but was also on the staff of a New York newspaper, and Claude told Kling the whole story. Kling immediately called the director of the hospital and told this administrator to check out the story with the German refugee doctor and call him back or he was going to release the story to the press.

The director called back and said according to Kling:

"Mr. Kling, to my regret, what you heard is true. We are bringing this doctor up on charges. We will move her into a private room and get the best doctor possible . . . anything you want!"

The director was horrified that a doctor would violate the Hippocratic Oath because he didn't like the political philosophies of his patient.

But both Geraldine and Claude Lightfoot had lost faith in the American medical profession because of this incident. They asked the Soviet Government for an examination at a Russian hospital. With Geraldine's good friend and nurse, Sylvia Woods, she traveled to the Soviet Union only to be told that nothing could be done. The Russian doctors advised her to return, and she died with friends and family in America in 1962.

112. ASHES OF JOE HILL (unmarked) (1882-1915)

Walk back to the Martyrs' Monument, and you are at the site where on May 1, 1916 some of the ashes of Joe Hill were scattered.

Joe Hill or Joseph Hillstrom was actually born, Joel Emmanuel Haagland in Sweden. He and his brother Paul came to America when Joe was only 19 years old, immediately after their parents death in 1901.

His first view of America was the poverty of New York City and its downtrodden, oppressed workers. His life is half myth and half fact, but his songs are still an inspiration to workers all over the world.

We do know some facts about his life. He learned English at the YMCA. He traveled all around the country for several years, and joined the Industrial Workers of the World in 1910. He was active in organizing dock workers around the port of San Pedro, and he took part in the San Diego "Free Speech Movement."

His songs included "Casey Jones-The Union Scab," which was written in 1911 during a shop workers strike on the Southern Pacific Railroad, and "The Preacher and the Slave" which is sometimes called "Pie in the Sky." He made fun of preachers like Dwight Moody and Billy Sunday who preached "pie in the sky religion" instead of "pie in the stomach now religion" (Note: It is ironic that the body of Billy Sunday, the evangelist of Sinclair Lewis' "Elmer Gantry," is buried in this cemetery just west and down the road from the Martyrs' Monument). Another of Joe Hill's songs "Rebel Girl" was inspired by Elizabeth Gurley Flynn (See No. 115).

In 1913, Hill helped to win an organizing strike of construction workers in Bingham, Utah. This particularly angered the Copper Trusts as well as the Mormon Church in Utah.

On Saturday, Jan. 10, 1914 at 10 p.m. two masked men entered the grocery store of J. C. Morrison. The robbers shot Morrison dead. When one of Morrison's sons wounded one of the robbers, the robbers killed him as well. A second son in hiding witnessed the whole thing.

When Joe Hill turned up at a doctor's office with a bullet wound it was reported to the police and he was arrested. He refused to tell where he got the wound or to give an alibi. He said a lady's honor was involved!

He was brought to trial on June 10, 1914 on a murder charge, found guilty and condemned to execution by a firing squad. From all over the world people came to his defence, refusing to believe he was guilty. Appeals were made to Woodrow Wilson by the Swedish government as well as by many distinguished Americans, but inspite of appeals the execution was carried out at 7:42 a.m. on November 19, 1915.

Hill had requested that he should not be buried in Utah and so his body was brought to Chicago. On November 23 members of the Industrial Workers of the World carried his body from the train station to Florence's Funeral Home at Racine and Taylor Streets. On Thanksgiving Day, November 25, 1915 a giant funeral was held at the West Side Auditorium (near Racine and Taylor) with over 5,000 people filling the hall and people standing in the streets for blocks around singing his songs. After the funeral his body was taken to Graceland Cemetery (Clark and Irving) where it was cremated on November 26. His remains were placed in envelopes, one for every state of the union except Utah. Envelopes were also sent to South America, Europe, Asia, South Africa, New Zealand, and Australia. All the ashes were to be scattered to the wind on May Day, 1916. The envelope for Illinois was scattered at the Martyrs' Monument.

The life of Joe Hill and his legend have inspired many literary works. You may be interested in reading some of them. Philip Foner wrote the book "The Case of Joe Hill." A play was written by Barrie Stavis titled "The Man Who Never Died." In 1969, Gibbs Smith published for the University of Utah Press the book "Joe Hill." "The Preacher and The Slave" by Wallace Stegner is a fictional novel based on the life of Joe Hill. Carl Sandburg wrote of Hill and folk singer Joe Glazer cut a record entitled "Songs of Joe Hill." In 1972 the motion picture "Joe Hill" was released and many more people learned of his songs, writings, and legend.

113. ASHES OF WILLIAM HAYWOOD (unmarked) (1869-1928)

After the death of William Haywood in Moscow in 1928 he asked that his body be cremated and half his ashes should be scattered at the site of the Martyrs' Monument. The other half are in the Kremlin Wall near Lenin's Tomb.

William Dudley Haywood, who was better known as "Big Bill" to millions of Americans was born in Salt Lake City. As a boy of nine he lost an eye in an accident with a slingshot; but this did not stop him from going to work as a miner shortly afterwards.

When he was 17 the Haymarket Affair took place, and he discussed the case with a fellow Irish worker, Pat Reynolds, who had been a member of the Knights of Labor. From Pat Reynolds he learned the meaning of trade unionism and the significance of what was happening during the Haymarket Trial.

In his twenties he married Nevada Jane Minor, became a cowboy and homesteader and continued mining. They had two daughters, but the marriage was not a happy one. Nevada Jane became ill, turned to religion, and never understood her husband's labor activities.

In 1896, Haywood became a charter member of the militant Western Federation of Miners (WFM). For the next decade Haywood assumed leadership of what was a class war between the mine owners and the union miners. The goals of Haywood and the WFM were the end of child labor, payment in money instead of company script, higher pay for dangerous work, and the end of company guards. In 1901, Haywood became a hero to workers all over America because the WFM won its battle against the mine owners through the help of a former union man who was Lt. Governor of Colorado. But in 1903, the Colorado Mine Owners' Association spent a great deal of money and defeated the friendly Lt. Governor and elected anti-union Governor Peabody. The militia were called out against the union men. The militia leaders were excessively violent and reportedly said: "To Hell with the Constitution . . . we are following the orders of Governor Peabody."

Because of lack of support from the AFL in his struggles for the miners, Haywood threw himself into the organization of a new labor movement. He became one of the leaders at the founding convention of the Industrial Workers of the World in Chicago in 1905 (See No. 30).

On December 20, 1905, former Governor Frank Steunenberg of Idaho was murdered and the WFM was blamed. Haywood and two other officers of the WFM, Moyer and Pettibone, were kidnapped without the use of extradition and taken to Idaho to stand trial for the murder. Eugene Debs said about their arrest and trial:

"There have been twenty years of revolutionary education, agitation, and organization since the Haymarket tragedy, and if an attempt is made to repeat it, there will be a revolution and I will do all in my power to precipitate it . . . If they attempt to murder Moyer, Haywood, and their brothers, a million revolutionists at least will meet them with guns."

Clarence Darrow was hired to defend Haywood and the others. Darrow won the case but Haywood had spent an entire year in jail.

In 1912, the IWW launched a great organizational drive as well as its "Free Speech Movement." Haywood came to the aid of the foreign, unskilled textile workers of Lawrence, Massachusetts, and they won their strike after nearly a quarter million workers throughout the East walked off their jobs. But the 1913 strikes at Paterson, New Jersey among silk mill workers and at Akron, Ohio among rubber workers ended in defeat for Haywood.

Since the IWW was against World War I, the Justice Department in September of 1917 launched full-scale raids against them across the country. The national headquarters of the organization on Madison Street in Chicago were raided and Haywood was arrested. Haywood and 105 others were sent to the notorious Cook County Jail (See No. 23) and placed in the same cells that had once held the Haymarket Martyrs. The next six months in this jail, living amid squalor and disease, completely broke his health. Haywood and 96 others were found guilty by Judge Landis (later to become baseball commissioner) and Haywood was to receive 20 years in Leavenworth Penitentiary and a fine of $30,000. While on bail, he toured the country to try to raise money to help jailed IWW members but was arrested whenever he tried to speak.

In the Spring of 1921, while awaiting his appeal to the Supreme Court, he jumped bail and went to Europe. He arrived in the Soviet Union on May Day and was greeted by Lenin and thousands of Russians cheered him in Red Square.

Lenin placed him in charge of the Kuzbas coal-mining colony in the Donets Basin, but his health wouldn't allow him to continue working. He came to live at the Lux Hotel in Moscow where he drank a great deal and was often visited by American friends who would drink with him and sing songs by Joe Hill and others from the "Little Red Song Book" of the IWW. During his remaining years he worked on the book, "The Autobiography of William D. Haywood" as well as articles on the Soviet Union for American magazines. In the spring of 1928 he had a stroke, and he died on May 18. Following his request he was cremated and half of his ashes were brought here to Waldheim to be placed beside the Haymarket Martyrs whose fate had first prompted his interest in the problems of American workers.

114. GRAVE OF NINA VAN ZANDT SPIES (Unmarked to the left of the Martyrs' Monument)

Nina Van Zandt became the "Rebel" of the 1880's when she fell in love with and later married August Spies.

Her full name was Rosanina Clarke Van Zandt and her father owned his own pharmaceutical company on South Water Street. Their home on Huron and Rush was plush (See No. 31 for more information on Nina). She had attended Miss Grant's Finishing School, and she graduated from Vassar College in 1883. Nina was slated to inherit nearly half a million dollars from an aunt in the East, who expected her to join society and make a "good" marriage.

Nina, like many Chicago society girls in July of 1886, decided to attend the Haymarket Trial for the fun of it. It was the thing to do that summer. Describing her first visit to the trial she said:

"I was expecting to see a rare collection of stupid, vicious, and criminal-looking men . . . But I was greatly surprised to find that several of them, so far from corresponding with this description, had intelligent, kindly, and good faces."

One day, on impulse, she decided to visit the men in their cells and she met Spies. Since the prisoners were writing their life stories to raise money to fight their case, Nina offered to help Spies with his autobiography. Their literary efforts together turned to love. Nina later said:

Nina Van Zandt in 1886

"My sympathy with the persecuted and lawlessly adjudicated prisoners soon changed into a feeling of amity for Mr. Spies . . . and from this feeling of friendship gradually developed a strong affection."

Nina had attracted the attention of newspapers throughout the trial. She came both in the morning and the afternoon to the trial, and twice a day she changed her gowns. She always wore a new one and they were always stunning. People wanted to read each day about what she was wearing, about her romance with Spies. A wax museum even put her image on display. Nina sued and forced the museum owners to pay her a fee for the use of the image, and she gave the money to the defense of the Haymarket Eight.

As the time for the execution approached, Nina was told she could not visit Spies any longer since she was not related or his wife. She and Spies then decided to get married, but the officials wouldn't let the ceremony take place in the jail. A friend of Spies suggested that they should use the device of a proxy marriage, which was held outside the jail with Spies' brother representing him.

In her later years Nina and Lucy Parsons marched together in many union and civil rights demonstrations. Nina was reduced to poverty after the death of her family, having been disinherited by her aunt. She lived in an old house on Morgan Street at the present site of the University of Illinois' Circle Campus for many years with dozens of cats, dogs, and even a horse in the house with her. She had asked Lucy Parsons to speak at her funeral when she died, and Lucy did this after her death in April of 1936.

Lucy Parsons was furious when she found Nina was not completely poverty stricken, since she left $3,000 in her will to former dancer Irene Castle's retreat for animals called "Orphans of the Storm." Lucy felt Nina should have left the money to the cause of American workers and toward the upkeep of the Martyrs' Monument.

Since there was no money left for a stone to mark her grave, Irving Abrams asked Irene Castle if some of the money given to her organization couldn't be used to mark the grave, but Miss Castle refused.

115. GRAVE OF ELIZABETH GURLEY FLYNN (1890-1964)

The beautiful and militant, Gurley Flynn, was the inspiration for Joe Hill's song "Rebel Girl." Her autobiography called, Rebel Girl, is still widely read and available in paperback.

She was born in Concord, New Hampshire on Aug. 7, 1890 of a poor family. Her father was active in the labor movement and her mother was a suffragette. The poverty of the textile workers in the area of New Hampshire had a profound effect on her life. In 1900, the family moved to South Bronx in New York City. In grammar school she joined a debating society and won a gold medal at her graduation in 1904. In 1906 she began to speak at Socialist street meetings and was arrested for the first time in the summer of that year. She also joined the IWW in 1907.

During the next ten years as a labor organizer and agitator she participated in free-speech struggles and mass strikes that made labor history, including the Lawrence Strike and the Paterson Strike. She worked with such prominent Socialists as William Haywood and Eugene V. Debs.

Elizabeth Gurley Flynn "The Rebel Girl"

After the Palmer Raids she organized defense for those arrested and became a founder of the American Civil Liberties Union in 1920.

She had been married in 1908 to an ore miner named John A. Jones and they had one son, Fred, who died in 1940. She divorced Jones in 1920. From 1913 to 1925 she lived and worked with Carlo Tresca, an Italian anarcho-syndicalist.

In 1937 she joined the Communist Party of the United States. In 1953 she was convicted under the Smith Act and received a three year jail term. This was at the time of the Joe McCarthy "Witch Hunts."

In 1961 she became Chairman of the Communist Party after the death of Eugene Dennis (See No. 118). That same year she was invited by Khrushchev to the Soviet Union but found she could not return to the U.S. because of visa problems with the State Department. She became ill and died in Moscow. On Sept. 7, 1964 her remains were cremated, and she was given a funeral with full Soviet State honors with Mr. and Mrs. Khrushchev and all government officials present. Her ashes were then returned to America to be buried here.

116. GRAVE OF WILLIAM Z. FOSTER (1881-1961)

Foster was the son of a poor Irish railroad car washer. He was born in Taunton, Massachusetts, but grew up in the slums of Philadelphia. At the age of seven he was forced to sell newspapers to contribute to the family income, and by nine he was working at the Wanamaker Department store. At ten he was apprenticed to an artist to learn the art of modeling and stonecutting but he left it when he was 13. For the next ten years he did dozens of different things and traveled all over the world. He tells about this in his book, "Pages From A Worker's Life."

Foster played a vital part in numerous strikes in a variety of industries. He worked with the IWW, the AFL, the Railroad Brotherhood, the C.I.O., and various independent unions. He also established the International Trade Union Educational League in 1916 and tried to organize the more radical workers into a militant force to change the AFL.

In 1917, William Z. Foster worked with many of the people that are buried around him in the organization of the packinghouse workers in Chicago and throughout the country. This was the first mass production industry to be successfully organized on a national scale. This was particularly difficult because of the diverse ethnic and racial mix of these workers who for generations had been played against each other by the great meat companies.

The Chicago labor movement had always been more militant than the national AFL and working with John Fitzpatrick of the Chicago Federation of Labor, Foster launched a campaign to organize steelworkers across the nation but especially in

William Z. Foster

South Chicago, Gary and Hammond. Samuel Gompers came to Chicago for a planning session at the Morrison Hotel (now the site of the First National Bank Building) and Gompers reluctantly backed the campaign because of Fosters' success in the meat industry.

Foster's organization of steel went very well at first, and again he showed great ability to reach Black and foreign speaking workers, but this was the period of Attorney General A. Mitchell Palmer's "Red Raids." The Steel Strike of 1919 was attacked in the anti-labor press as a "Red menace."

Foster was brought before a Senate Committee and his earlier writings, especially on syndicalism and worker control of industry were used against him. Instead of the Senate investigating the conditions in the steel industry and the problems of its workers, they investigated Foster. Samuel Gompers saw the bad press he was getting and deserted Foster. The steel companies finally agreed to the eight hour day, (steelworkers had been working 10-12 hours daily) but refused to recognize the union, and the strike collapsed.

Foster was very bitter. Fitzpatrick and the Chicago Federation of Labor employed him for a short time as a writer for their newspaper, but in November 1920 Foster formed the Trade Union Educational League (TUEL). The TUEL was an attempt to get labor's story across to the workers, since Foster felt that his failure in 1919 was partly due to a lack of education and communication among workers.

From 1926 to 1928 Foster worked with the United Mine Workers, and he was active in the 1931 coal strike.

Foster had become a member of the Communist Party in 1921, and he was arrested for attending a meeting in Bridgman, Michigan of the party. He was indicted for something called "criminal syndicalism," but he was freed because the jury could not agree on the verdict. New Republic magazine said that "it may be that the result of the Michigan Trial is after all a victory for the people."

Foster was the Communist candidate for President of the United States in 1924, 1928, and 1932. Although the Communist Party was dissolved during W.W. II, Foster helped to reestablish it after the war. Foster disagreed sharply with the "Cold War Policies" of the Truman Administration. He declared that the Administration would "precipitate civil war" in China unless it removed American troops and withdrew its backing of Chiang Kai-shek's "shaky regime."

Foster wrote six books. One of these, "From Bryan to Stalin," the Saturday Review described as "a creditable piece of biographical writing, frank, clear, and complete."

Foster was described by Current Opinion magazine "an incurable romantic" and "a hard fighter, whose zeal and self-sacrificial devotion to his cause cannot be questioned."

He died on September 1, 1961.

117. RAYMOND HANSBROUGH (1903-1950)

Raymond Hansbrough was originally a steelworker on Chicago's southside. In the 1930's and 40's he became a leader of the Chicago Communist Party working with Blacks from his office on 43rd Street. He also was active in working with people in the field of art and drama.

He was actively involved in the 1930's in the nationwide campaign to free the Nine Scottsboro Boys who were brought to trial on rape charges and were to be executed. He was also involved in the Angelo Herndon case in which a Black youth was charged with "incitement to insurrection" because he dared to lead a demonstration of white and Black unemployed in Georgia.

In the 1940's he left Chicago for New York City to work for the Black Liberation Committee. He was married to Amelia Ferguson, who was a civil rights leader.

His pioneer work in civil rights is the reason for the inscription on his plaque "A Selfless Devotion to the Liberation of the Oppressed."

118. EUGENE DENNIS (1904-1961)

Eugene Dennis was born in Seattle, Washington on August 10, 1904. His real name was Francis Eugene Waldron. He went to the University of Washington for a time, and then went to sea as a sailor. He had great energy and was a brilliant speaker at rallies. In early 1928 he joined the Young Communist League in Seattle. On Sept. 24, 1928 he married Regina (Peggy) Karaciek, and a year later on Nov. 30, 1929 in Los Angeles they had a son Timothy Waldron.

In 1930, Dennis led several unemployment marches and was arrested by the police on charges that he was "inciting to riot" and engaged in "criminal syndicalism."

Between 1930 and 1934, Dennis and his wife Peggy visited Germany, France, England, South Africa, and the Soviet Union. While in Russia he was asked to go to China. He and his wife left their baby, Timothy, with a Russian family. While in China, Dennis worked with the Maoist army against Chiang-Kai-Shek.

When they returned to Russia, they found their child had become very attached to his Russian family and like Paul Robeson, they decided it would be best to have their child raised in the Soviet Union. When they returned to America, they had another son, but continued to write to Timothy until W.W. II started and they lost all contact.

In 1937, Dennis became State Secretary of the Communist Party of Wisconsin and later was elected General Secretary of the Communist Party of the United States. In 1947, during the "Red Scare" that followed the Second World War, Dennis was brought before the House Committee on Un-American Activities headed by Rep. J. Parnell Thomas, later proved guilty of stealing government funds. Dennis dramatically presented his case to the Committee with the statements:

"This Committee . . . has arrogated to itself repressive powers specifically forbidden by the Bill of Rights.

"Today the American people understand how truly Thoreau spoke when he said, 'They are the lovers of law and order who uphold the law when the government breaks it.'"

Dennis eventually went to a federal prison in 1950, but he wrote a book entitled, "Ideas They Cannot Jail," (1950), and later another entitled "Letters From Prison (1956)." When Dennis left jail it was discovered he had cancer, and the doctors gave him very little hope.

When Khrushchev visited the United States in 1959 during the Eisenhower Administration, on the very day that Khrushchev was to appear before the United Nations, Dennis was sent an invitation to visit the Soviet delegation.

Khrushchev greeted him warmly and then Khrushchev said he wished him to meet someone else who was in the other room. That "someone" turned out to be his son, Timothy, who was now a Soviet scientist, and writer for Pravda. Khrushchev had especially selected him as one of his translators so that father and son could be reunited.

Khrushchev had also brought with him two top cancer specialists . . . one Czech and the other Russian, who examined Dennis to see if anything could be done to save his life. When Dennis finally died in 1962, his Russian raised son came to the United States again to attend the funeral.

119. JACK JOHNSTONE (1881-1942)

Johnstone was born in Scotland, and as a very young man he served in the Boer War in South Africa. He then came to live in British Columbia and in 1912 helped to found the Syndicalist League of North America, especially Lodge No. 1 in Nelson, British Columbia. In Nelson the more radical Syndicalist group controlled the AFL.

Johnstone then came to the United States in 1915 and to Chicago where the Chicago Federation of Labor (CFL) was considered so radical by the AFL that it had lost its charter several times. Johnstone was employed by the Chicago Federation of Labor and the Illinois Federation as a paid organizer. He helped to found the Stock Yards Labor Council on July 25, 1917 and signed up nearly 40,000 workers by November of that same year.

During World War I, he organized and struck 3,000 stockhandlers working for the Union Stockyards & Transit Company. Although he and William Z. Foster were threatened with jail terms by Mr. Claybaugh of the Department of Justice, they stood firm, signed with the company, and won.

Johnstone believed in a policy called "boring from within" to make conservative unions more responsive to the needs of their members. Many foreign and black workers were reluctant to join the AFL but Johnstone produced what the papers called the "Checkerboard Parade," black and white workers joining together; and this was at the time of the "race riots" (July, 1919) in Chicago. Over 200,000 workers eventually joined some dozen unions in the meat industry across the country . . . these included ethnic workers, 25,000 Blacks, office workers, and even stockyards police. But fighting between unions, the hostility of management, and the murder of two organizers led to the collapse of Johnstone's organizing campaign in 1921.

Johnstone assisted William Z. Foster in the Steel Strike of 1919. When Foster joined the Communist Party, Johnstone also joined. Johnstone worked with the Trade Union Educational League in the 1920's, and he was arrested in Chicago in August of 1922 for his organizing work. Johnstone served on a Committee for the Recognition of the Soviet Union and for Russian Relief during the 1920's.

As the Great Depression hit America, there was the feeling that political differences should be set aside by labor for the general good and Johnstone served on the Executive Board of the Trade Union Unity League to try to work with the AFL. During May of 1931, he was busy organizing miners, and in 1933, he led a strike of 65,000 workers in New York City.

In the early 1930's he went to India to work with Ghandi. He was arrested by the British and would have been executed except for an international protest campaign. World pressure finally forced the British to release him.

Even in his last years he was busy organizing miners and steelworkers in Western Pennsylvania.

When he died in 1942, a giant funeral was held for him in the Ashland Auditorium (See No. 94). The Chicago Federation of Labor sent an official delegate to pay respect to this man who had organized so many Chicago workers.

120. GRAVE AND MONUMENT TO EMMA GOLDMAN
(June 29, 1869-May 14, 1940)

(Although the year 1939 appears on the monument this is incorrect. She died in Canada in 1940)

A noted anarchist lecturer and publicist, an agitator for free speech and a popularizer of the arts, a leading feminist and a pioneer advocate of birth control, a sharp critic of Soviet Communism and an untiring supporter of the Catalonian revolutionists during the Spanish Civil War, Emma Goldman was one of the most exciting and influential women in American history.

Emma was the "Angela Davis" of her day. She and one of her early lovers, Alexander Berkman, purchased the gun that would later be used in Berkman's attempted assassination of Frick, manager of Andrew Carnegie's Homestead Mills at the time of the Homestead Strike. She served one year in prison, but that year changed Emma's attitude toward the use of violence to change society.

Emma had hated oppression in Russia where she was born and she was horrified by the hanging of Parsons, Spies, Fischer, and Engel. On the evening of Nov. 11, 1887, Emma Goldman and her sister Helena, who was quietly weeping, walked over to their parents' house. Inside there was much excited discussion of the executions.

A woman laughed: "What's all this lament about? The men were murderers. It is well they were hanged."

Emma leaped for the woman's throat. Pulled back, she snatched up a pitcher of water from the table and threw its contents in the woman's face. "Out," she cried, "Out, or I will kill you!" As the frightened woman hastened out Emma fell to the floor, crying hysterically. She had thought she had left such oppression and injustice behind in Russia and now she saw it in America and in Buffalo, N.Y. where she first lived.

Emma's lecture to Roger Baldwin, a conservative Harvard graduate, changed his thinking and led him to found the American Civil Liberties Union.

Among Emma's friends and admirers were Jane Addams, John Dewey, Bertrand Russell, and Charles and Mary Beard.

Her greatest enemy was J. Edgar Hoover, who along with Attorney-General Palmer had her deported in 1919. Hoover called her and Berkman "beyond doubt two of the most dangerous anarchists in this country and if permitted to return to the community will result in undue harm."

She was only allowed to return to the United States once in 1935 when hundreds of people had to be turned away from a dinner in her honor at the Waldorf-Astoria Hotel in New York. Her greatest moment was when thousands of Spaniards greeted her in Barcelona when that city was held by the workers during the Spanish Civil War. They saw her as an inspiration and greeted her as one of their own.

A number of excellent books about her life are available including her two volume autobiography, "My Life," and "Rebel in Paradise" by Richard Drennon.

In death she asked that her remains be returned to America to rest beside the Haymarket Martyrs that had inspired her life.

121. PETIS PERRY (1897-1965)

Although Petis Perry was poor and Black and never had more than a third grade education, he taught himself to read and write. He worked in Los Angeles with the Communist Party in the early 1930's. As a Black man, he fought for other Black men including the Scottsboro Boys.

Long before the Civil Rights Marches of the 1960's, Perry wrote a pamphlet entitled "Negro Representation." Later, he moved from Los Angeles to New York City where he headed the Commission on Black Liberation of the Communist Party.

During the time of the Smith Act, which outlawed the Communist Party, and the "Witch-hunts" of the Joe McCarthy era, Perry was one of the few Communist leaders who did not go "underground." His philosophy until his death was: . . . "Black and White-Unite and Fight."

122. ESTHER FOSTER (Died 1965)

Born Esther Abramowitz in the old Russian province of Kovno, she came to the United States in her girlhood and became a New York City clothing worker. She worked in a factory under sweatshop conditions, and she came to admire the anarchist cause. She married young and had three children, Rebecca, Sylvia, and David by her first husband. In 1912, she married William Z. Foster and joined the Foster group in the Socialist Party. For the rest of her life she worked with her husband who is buried close by. Foster wrote the following in one of his books:

"All her adult life she has been most ardent revolutionist. She is one of those to whom the workers' struggle is the very breath of life . . . An intelligent and devoted comrade, she has been my constant companion and a tower of strength to me in all my labor activities for these many years."

123. JACK STACHEL (1900-1965)

Stachel's career was in the garment industry in New York and as a youth he experienced the sweat-shop conditions in that industry. At 19, he became a charter member of the Communist Party and was an active member of the Young Communist League as well as a national educational director. In 1926, he was active in the New York Garment Workers strike. In the early 1930's he led one of the first marches on Washington D.C. against the depression policies of Hoover's administration, and he became an organizer of Unemployed Councils that later took part in the Bonus March on Washington in 1932. He was arrested in Detroit on May 26, 1930 for demonstrating against unemployment in that city.

Later in 1932, he was invited by the Soviet Government to attend Lenin University in Moscow, and he helped to work out a compromise between students and the administration during a riot at that university.

After his return to America he became Executive Secretary

of the Communist Party at a time when the Trade Union Unity League was working very closely with the A.F. of L. to organize workers. Later he worked with the C.I.O. to organize all kinds of workers in Pennsylvania, Ohio, Indiana, and autoworkers in Michigan. Stachel once said that workers believed the promises of Roosevelt and "took seriously" the statement that they had the right "to join unions of their choice." However, everywhere employers were trying to fight unionism or killing workers as they did at the Memorial Day Massacre in Chicago in 1937. Jack Stachel later became Organizational Secretary of the Communist Party and he and his wife Bertha were active until his death in New York City in 1965. Bertha is still alive. His family wanted him to be buried close to Foster, Dennis, and all the others he had worked with throughout his life.

124. ALEXANDER L. TRACHTENBERG (1885-1966)

The young Trachtenberg was a student at Yale at the time that W.E.B. DuBois was a professor there, and the rest of his life was influenced by the teachings of DuBois.

He graduated from Yale with a Doctor of Philosophy degree and taught at the Rand School in New York with the historians Charles and Mary Beard. He also worked for the International Lady Garment Workers for some time.

He was at first an active member of the Socialist Party but in 1919 became a charter member of the Communist Party.

Alexander Trachtenberg would become the founder of International Publishers which is still in operation today, and which distributed books by Flynn, Foster, Marx, Lenin and also on every subject imaginable. Trachtenberg not only sold books, but he also wrote several including "The History of Legislation for the Protection of Coal Miners in Pennsylvania, 1824-1915," and "Karl Marx and Fredrick Engels: Letters to Americans 1848-1895." With his academic background it was natural that Trachtenberg was involved in writing and education. During the McCarthy Era of the early 1950's, like the Haymarket martyrs, Trachtenberg was jailed not for what he did but for what he was writing about. It is ironic that one of his pamphlets was on the origins of May Day and the Haymarket Affair.

Harvey M. Matusow, also an employee of the Department of Justice, confessed in his memoirs, called "False Witness," that he had been instrumental in convicting a score of persons, Communist and non-Communist as well as trade union leaders on perjury testimony bought and paid for by the government. Federal Judge Dimmock formally found that Matusow had lied in testifying that Trachtenberg had advocated the violent overthrow of the government. Judge Dimmock granted the Communist leader a new trial and he was freed.

Now he lies with the Haymarket Martyrs and all those in Waldheim, who in different ways tried to fight for freedom of speech and expression.

Through Haymarket Revisited and your tour of these sites we hope the significance and importance of these basic American Freedoms has been spotlighted. You may not agree with all the things that the people buried here did in their lifetime, but one must realize that in a "free society" all must have the right to express their ideas and philosophies of life.

TIME LINE

1855
April 21: "Lager Beer Riot"... German and other foreign born citizens are denied city jobs. Beer gardens and saloons are closed in order to deny them freedom of speech and assembly. They march on City Hall. City uses police and vigilante committee against them and Steve Martin is killed and many wounded.

1867
May 1: "Eight Hour Day Strike"... Chicago workers led by the Molders Union try to get employers to obey a law passed in March of 1867 for eight hours to be the "legal work day in the State of Illinois."

1869
The Knights of Labor are organized in Philadelphia, and the organization quickly spreads to Chicago.

1871
Oct. 8-9: "Chicago Fire"... People all over the world donate 5 million dollars for the relief of the workers of the city. Mayor Medill gives the money to the Relief and Aid Society made up of his business friends.

1872
Winter: "The Bread Riots"... Thousands of poor demand aid from the Relief and Aid Society but instead they are driven into the LaSalle Street Tunnel and clubbed and beaten by the police.

1873
January: Albert and Lucy Parsons arrived in Chicago. Parsons discovers the rich businessmen of Chicago have been borrowing from the Relief and Aid funds instead of giving them to the poor.

1874
Jan. 1: Workingmen's Party of Illinois organized to protest unemployment and lack of relief funds.

1876
July 4: "American Centennial"-Albert Parsons is a delegate to the Philadelphia Convention to form the Workingmen's Party of the United States.

1877
July 23: "Railroad Strike of 1877" reaches Chicago and Parsons speaks in the Market Square and is fired and "blacklisted" the next day.
July 26: "Battle of the Viaduct"-U.S. Troops of the Second Militia Regiment and police attack about 5,000 workers at Halsted and 16th Street. "Turner Hall Raid"-Police raid the hall during a meeting of the German Furniture Workers, kill Mr. Tessman, wound many others. A judge later finds the police guilty of preventing the workers from having their right to freedom of speech and assembly.

1879
March 22: "Rally at Exposition Hall"-40,000 people come to hear Spies and Parsons speak. Money is raised for workers newspapers, and new worker military groups drill.
April: Illinois General Assembly outlaws workers' military groups. Only police and business dominated State Militia may drill and carry guns.

1880
<u>August</u>: Frank Stauber is not seated as city alderman for the 14th Ward after ballot stuffing of the year before. Parsons had the same thing happen to him earlier in the 15th Ward. Workers became discouraged with the democratic process.

1881
<u>April</u>: Strike at Crane factory.

1882
The Federation of Organized Trades and Labor Union, later known as the A.F. of L., is founded by Samuel Gompers.

1884
<u>Summer</u>: The American Federation of Labor meets in Chicago and declares that May 1, 1886 will be the day for workers all over America to demand the eight hour day.
<u>Nov. 25</u>: "Poor Peoples March"-Thousands of poor workers in Chicago follow Lucy and Albert Parsons by the homes of the richest people in the city demanding food and jobs.

1885
<u>April 28</u>: "March Against the Board of Trade"-In protest to the opening of their new building and price-fixing of grain and other foods thousands of workers march.
<u>July</u>: "Street Car Strike"-Workers clubbed and killed by police and Pinkerton Detectives. Bonfield issues "shoot to kill order" against orders of Mayor Harrison.

1886
<u>May 1</u>: "Eight Hour Day Movement" begins and a week of activities is planned. 80,000 workers led by Albert, Lucy Parsons, and their children march up Michigan Avenue.
<u>May 2</u>: Sunday . . . The downtown area is empty except for 35,000 workers marching through Grant Park.
<u>May 3</u>: Monday . . . Spies speaks at lumber workers meeting and sees Bonfield attack workers at the nearby McCormick Reaper Plant. Spies demands worker action. Engel and Waller at Grief's Hall suggest a meeting in Haymarket Square for the next day to protest police brutality.
<u>May 4</u>: "Haymarket Protest Meeting"-Tuesday evening at 8:30 P.M., Spies opens the meeting of 2,500 people. By 10:25 with only 200 people remaining Fielden is just closing the meeting when 176 policemen attack the audience and a bomb is thrown by someone unknown.
<u>May 5</u>: Inspector Bonfield and Captain Schaack begin arrests of the Haymarket Eight and close down all union newspapers, end freedom of speech and assembly in Chicago, and declare martial law.
The Jewish community tries to protest rats, garbage, and bad housing and unaware of Haymarket or the declaration of martial law they are clubbed and beaten by the police at the Van Buren Street bridge.
<u>June 21</u>: Haymarket Trial begins and Parsons turns himself in.
<u>July 15</u>: The jury is finally selected and State's Attorney Grinnel opens the case for the prosecution.
<u>July 31</u>: Defense attorneys Black, Zeisler, and Salomon open the case for the Haymarket Eight.
<u>Aug. 20</u>: The Jury reports its verdict of guilty with the death penalty by hanging for seven of the Haymarket Eight and 15 years at hard labor for Neebe.

<u>Oct. 7-9</u>: Haymarket Eight allowed to respond in court to the verdict.
<u>Dec. 3</u>: Date for the hanging originally given by Judge Gary. This was delayed because of an appeal to the Illinois Supreme Court.

1887

<u>March 18</u>: Illinois Supreme Court finally hears the appeal of the Haymarket case.
<u>Sept. 2</u>: Illinois Supreme Court upholds the conviction.
<u>Sept. 16</u>: Samuel Gompers and the A.F. of L. pass a resolution protesting the hanging.
<u>Oct. 29</u>: Members of the French Chamber of Deputies in Paris protest the execution to the Governor of Illinois.
<u>Oct</u>: Ft. Highland (later Ft. Sheridan) established as a permanent military base to protect Chicago against future labor troubles.
<u>Nov. 2</u>: The appeal to the U.S. Supreme Court in Washington is denied.
<u>Nov. 6</u>: English workers in 49 cities protest the execution. Oscar Wilde, George Bernard Shaw, and Prince Peter Kropotkin, circulate petitions and lead mass marches in London.
<u>Nov. 10</u>: Samuel Gompers comes to Springfield to see the Governor and protest the execution. Fielden and Schwab have their sentences changed to life imprisonment instead of death by the Governor. Lingg is found in his cell with his head half blown off and he dies in the afternoon.
<u>Nov. 11</u>: Parsons, Spies, Fischer, and Engel are executed at noon.
<u>Nov. 13</u>: The funeral takes place down Milwaukee Avenue and to downtown Chicago and then out to Waldheim.

1888

<u>Oct</u>: Lucy Parsons sails for England on speaking tour to get support for pardoning of Fielden, Schwab, and Neebe from jail.

1889

<u>Jan</u>: The Chicago Times exposes police corruption, especially involving Bonfield and Schaack, and they are later removed from the police force.
<u>May 30</u>: The Police Monument is unveiled in the Haymarket Square.
<u>July 14</u>: "May Day"-adopted as an International workers' day in Paris at the Centennial of the French Revolution to honor the "Martyrs of Chicago."

1893

<u>June 25</u>: The Martyrs' Monument in Waldheim Cemetery is unveiled.
<u>June 26</u>: John Peter Altgeld pardons Neebe, Fielden and Schwab.

1905

<u>Nov.</u>: The Industrial Workers of the World are founded in Chicago with Lucy Parsons as one of the founding members.

1915

<u>Nov.</u>: Joe Hill is executed in Salt Lake City and brought to Chicago for a giant funeral. His ashes are later scattered at the Martyrs' Monument.

1922
<u>Feb. 7</u>: Samuel Fielden became the last of the Haymarket Eight to die at his ranch in La Veta, Colorado.

1939
<u>June 22</u>: Lucy Parsons speaks at the old McCormick plant, where Spies spoke in 1886, asking them to organize.

1942
<u>March 7</u>: Lucy Parsons dies in a fire in her home.

1968
<u>May 2</u>: The Illinois Labor History Society held a memorial rally in honor of workers killed in Haymarket Square.

1969
<u>Oct. 6</u>: The Police Monument is blown up for the first time.

1970
<u>May 3</u>: The State Historical Society and Illinois Labor History Society place an historical marker in Haymarket Square.
<u>May 4</u>: The Police Monument is replaced for the first time.
<u>Oct. 6</u>: The Police Monument is blown up for the second time.

1971
<u>Jan. 5</u>: The Police Monument is replaced for the second time.
<u>May 2</u>: The Martyrs' Monument becomes the property of the Illinois Labor History Society.

1972
<u>Feb.</u>: The Police Monument is removed from Haymarket Square to Central Police Headquarters, and the Illinois Labor History Society recommends it be replaced by a monument to the eight hour day, freedom of speech, and freedom of assembly.

READING LIST

You might enjoy reading one of these books about the Haymarket Incident and the Martyrs before or after you have taken the tour.

BARNARD, HARRY. **EAGLE FORGOTTEN: The Life of John Peter Altgeld.** Indianapolis: Bobbs-Merrill Charter Books, 1962. This excellent book on Altgeld contains a great deal of material on Haymarket. Chapters 11 through 13 deal with the Haymarket Meeting, the Trial, and the Execution. Chapters 20 through 26 deal with Altgeld's pardon of the three remaining Haymarket Martyrs.

BRECHER, JEREMY. **STRIKE.** San Francisco: Straight Arrow Books, 1972. This excellent new paperback tells the true story of American labor history from 1877-1972. Chapter II gives a brief but excellent summary of the Haymarket Affair.

CALMER, ALAN. **LABOR AGITATOR: The Story of Albert R. Parsons.** New York: International Publishers, 1937. This book depends a great deal on material from Lucy Parsons' book **The Life of Albert R. Parsons.** It is a short readable account of Parsons' role in the Haymarket Affair.

DAVID, HENRY. **THE HISTORY OF THE HAYMARKET AFFAIR.** New York: Farrar & Rinehart, 1936 (Revised 1958). The best and most thorough book on the events leading up to Haymarket, the event itself, the trial, and all of the effects it had on the history of labor.

FARR, FINIS. **CHICAGO: A Personal History of America's Most American City.** New Rochelle, New York: Arlington House, 1973. Although Chapter 5 and 6 deal briefly with the Railroad Strike of 1877 and Haymarket, the entire book gives you a behind the scenes view of Chicago's business leaders and what they were really like. It is a light reading, fun kind of book although the end of the book is weak compared with the excellent first half.

FAST, HAROLD. **The American: A Middlewestern Legend.** New York: Duell, Sloan, and Pearce, 1946. A novel based on Altgeld and his role in the Haymarket Affair.

FONER, PHILLIP S. **THE AUTOBIOGRAPHIES OF THE HAYMARKET MARTYRS.** New York: Humanities Press, 1969. With an introduction by Philip Foner this book is a collection of autobiographical sketches of the lives of the Haymarket Eight which originally appeared in the labor journal **Knights of Labor** between Oct. 16, 1886 and Oct. 8, 1887 along with comments by their attorney Capt. W. P. Black. Professor Foner also found a previously unpublished account of the life of Louis Lingg.

HARRIS, FRANK. **THE BOMB, A Novel.** Chicago: University of Chicago Press, 1920 (reissued 1963). This fictional novel by Frank Harris was condemned by Lucy Parsons as inaccurate since he has Schnaubelt dying in Bavaria confessing that he threw the bomb. Lucy claimed that Schnaubelt was still alive at that time in California. The other historical facts around the novel are accurate and it is well worth reading.

KOGAN, BERNARD R. **THE CHICAGO HAYMARKET RIOT; ANARCHY ON TRIAL.** Boston: Heath, 1959. This excellent collection of primary sources contains testimony from the trial from both the defense and prosecution, necessary background material by the author, and Altgeld's and Judge Gary's attitudes toward the trial.

LENS, SIDNEY. **THE LABOR WARS.** Garden City, New York: Doubleday, 1973. This book traces American labor history from the Molly Maguires to the Sit Downs of the 1930's. Chapter 4 deals briefly with Haymarket, but this excellent book throughout gives you a picture of the relationship of Haymarket to the rest of labor history.

LUM, DYER DANIEL. **THE GREAT TRIAL OF THE CHICAGO ANARCHISTS.** New York: Arno Press, 1969. This is a reprint of the original printed in 1886. Lum was a friend of the Parsons and contributed many articles to **The Alarm.**

MELTZER, MILTON. **BREAD AND ROSES.** New York: Alfred A. Knopf, 1967. This little paperback is excellent for junior high, high school, and adults on the period from 1865-1915. Chapter 11 tells the story of Haymarket.

NADEN, CORINNE J. **THE HAYMARKET AFFAIR, Chicago 1886.** New York: Franklin Watts, Inc. 1968. This illustrated, 55 page booklet dealing with labor background, the bomb, the trial, verdict, pardon, and aftermath is excellent for use in junior high school and high school classes to supplement the regular textbooks.

PARSONS, LUCY. **THE LIFE OF ALBERT R. PARSONS.** A rare book that still may be found in some libraries. Lucy originally wrote it in 1889 and put out many editions until her death in 1942.

ROGERS, DR. VINCENT R. **POLITICAL JUSTICE: THE HAYMARKET THREE.** Middletown, Conn.: American Education Publications (Xerox Corp.), 1972. This 48 page pamphlet is basically about Governor Altgeld pardoning of the three martyrs who were not executed. It is excellent for grades 7-12 and is available in quantity. It covers the Haymarket Meeting, the Trial, Altgeld, Public Relation to the Pardon. It then compares Haymarket to the Black Panther Trials of 1971.

SCHAACK, MICHAEL J. **ANARCHY AND ANARCHISTS.** Chicago: F. J. Schulte & Co., 1889. This rare book by Inspector Schaack of the Chicago Police Department is about one-third lies by his later admission. The propaganda is so obvious that one can easily separate it from some very interesting historical data. This book was used by the Pinkerton Detective Agency to promote business throughout the country.

WERSTEIN, IRVING. **STRANGLED VOICES; The Story of the Haymarket Affair.** New York: Macmillan, 1969.

WHEELOCK, LEWIS F. **URBAN PROTESTANT REACTIONS TO THE CHICAGO HAYMARKET AFFAIR.** 1886-1893. Unpublished Ph.D. dissertation, University of Iowa, 1950. This is valuable reading for scholars who wish to read sermons and articles expressing the thought of ministers and congregations toward the event, trial, execution and Altgeld pardon.

ZEISLER, ERNEST BLOOMFIELD. **THE HAYMARKET RIOT.** Chicago: Alexander J. Isaacs, 1956. A limited edition book by the son of the attorney of the "Haymarket Eight." Based on talks with his father and reports from Dr. Otto Schmidt, he concluded that Schnaubelt threw the bomb from the still standing weather-vestibule of the building at the northeast corner of Desplaines and Randolph.